DAILY THOUGHTS ON
BIBLE CHARACTERS

DAILY THOUGHTS
on Bible Characters

Harry Foster

VICTORY PRESS
London and Eastbourne

ISBNs: Hardback 085476 129 2
Paperback 085476 130 6

Printed in Great Britain for
VICTORY PRESS (Evangelical Publishers Ltd)
Lottbridge Drove, Eastbourne, Sussex
by Richard Clay (The Chaucer Press) Ltd,
Bungay, Suffolk

For all those words which were written long ago are meant to teach us today; that when we read in the Scriptures of the endurance of men and all the help that God gave them in those days, we may be encouraged to go on hoping in our own time.

Romans 15.4 (Phillips).

JANUARY 1st

AARON   *Reading: Hebrews 5. 1–4.*

Aaron was the first man chosen by God to make priestly sacrifices for sin on behalf of the people, yet even while the pattern of his beautiful garments was being revealed to Moses he was the very one who was leading the nation into deep sin. God would have been fully justified in disqualifying him from ever occupying the High Priestly position, but in abounding grace He not only forgave him but made him a minister of mercy to all other penitents. Surely whenever Aaron confessed the people's sins he must have remembered the shame of the golden calf and have been freshly grateful for God's great mercy to him personally. Grace makes a man a mighty intercessor. If the truth were told, the Israelites may have been more helped by Aaron's forgiven failure than by his beautiful robes.

JANUARY 2nd

ABEL   *Reading: Genesis 4. 1–10.*

The first physical death was caused not by the just wrath of God but by the wicked anger of a man. The first body laid in a grave was not that of Adam, the man who offended God, but of Abel, the man who pleased Him. It was not some outside enemy who detroyed the beautiful home-life of the first family but an envious member of that very family. Why do men blame God for human misery when it all springs from human folly? Even so God has not abandoned us, but to this day He continues to speak to men through this man's faith. For although Abel was murdered he is not silent. He speaks to us of a better sacrifice than his lamb, even the shed blood of the Lamb of God. If instead of blaming God men would listen to that voice, they would find the way into God's kingdom where there is no more anger and no more death.

JANUARY 3rd

ABIATHAR   *Reading: 1 Samuel 22. 20–23.*

"Fear not," said David to the priest Abiathar; "I will make Saul's hatred of you my responsibility. He hated me first; he only hates you because of me." David went on to assure the priest that he would find complete safety in keeping close to him. This proved true, for Abiathar was preserved throughout David's life-time, first during his rejection and then in his kingdom. "Fear not," the Lord Jesus said to His disciples; "if the world hate you, ye know that it hated me before it hated you." He also went on to assure us that if we keep close to Him we shall know perfect safety, and since He lives for ever our safety is eternal.

JANUARY 4th

ABIGAIL   *Reading: 1 Samuel 25. 18–31.*

Nabal was not the Lord's anointed, like Saul, but only a surly farmer whom everyone disliked. He so provoked David and his men that they were ready to kill him. It seemed that nothing could restrain David from committing this act which would have been a lasting reproach to his good name. But someone did. It was Abigail. She herself would have been glad to get rid of Nabal, yet she knew how wrong it is to take the law into one's own hands. "Wait for God," she pleaded with David. "Do not fight for yourself but leave your wrongs with Him." In less than two weeks David was to thank God with all his heart for this wise counsel. God dealt with Nabal, and David kept his hands clean. "Abigail" means "the father's delight". God is always delighted with patient faith.

JANUARY 5th

ABIJAH   *Reading: 1 Kings 14. 1–13.*

A child may have a very genuine experience of God. Abijah died young, but not before he had found acceptance through faith. His faith made him a different person from the rest of his family, for the Lord could not say a single word of good about the others. Death is a dark mystery, especially when it comes to the young, but one such as Abijah's helps to reconcile us to it. By his early death the boy was taken still unspoiled from his father's corrupt court to an incorruptible inheritance with God. Moreover he was sincerely mourned by all the people. It was better for Abijah to have had a short life and be honoured, than to have lived on and ended in disgrace like his father, Jeroboam.

JANUARY 6th

ABINADAB   *Reading: 1 Samuel 7. 1–12.*

Was it that King Saul could never be trusted with the Ark of the Covenant? One thing is certain, that throughout all his reign he had no association with it. Before he came to the throne it was safely sheltered in the house on the hill less than ten miles from Jerusalem where Abinadab lived, and there it stayed until long after Saul had perished. Only a man of a reverent disposition could have been entrusted with the custody of such a sacred vessel. Saul was not that kind of man. He was a man of moods—sometimes modest, often rash, and always self-willed. Abinadab, however, was a steady believer, a man who kept himself "in the fear of the Lord all the day long" (Proverbs 23.17). No doubt that was why God committed the Ark to his care until King David took over responsibility for it.

JANUARY 7th

ABISHAI   *Reading: 2 Samuel 21. 15–17.*

But for Abishai the story of David might have ended in tragedy. He who had begun by killing Goliath was now at the mercy of another giant, who welcomed the opportunity of using his new sword on the aged king. The now feeble David was waiting for the inevitable death blow when Abishai jumped forward, and added one more to the list of his courageous victories. David's fighting days were over; he had become a liability instead of an asset. Younger warriors are apt to despise the weaknesses of their ageing fellow believers. How much better it would be if, like Abishai, they fought their battles for them, and sheltered them with kindly consideration.

JANUARY 8th

ABNER   *Reading: 2 Samuel 3. 31–39.*

Probably for some time Abner felt that it was his duty to support the house of Saul; but at last, whether from disillusionment with Ish-bosheth or because he came to understand that David was really God's chosen king, he changed sides and was ready to bring about a reconciliation of the two parties under the single kingdom of David. The reconciliation took place, but Abner himself never profited from it, for treacherous Joab, nursing an old grievance and jealous for his own position, eliminated him. This brought peril and weakness to David's throne, and distress to his heart. Even an anointed ruler is weakened in his kingdom if his servants yield to spite and jealousy, and quarrel among themselves.

JANUARY 9th

ABRAHAM THE CITIZEN   *Reading: Hebrews 11. 8–16.*

Abraham was really a city man. He belonged to the finest and most modern city of his day, and when he left Ur it was because he was promised a place in an even better city. This promise has not yet been implemented, but it will be when the holy city of light comes down out of heaven from God. Abraham could only see that city by faith, but the sight was so wonderful, even from a distance, that he was ready to put up with temporary tent life while he waited for his new citizenship. What did he give up? A place in a city which would have sunk into complete oblivion if modern archaeologists had not got busy on its ruins. What will he gain? A place in God's own city which has eternal foundations and everlasting glory. This prospect made tent life tolerable.

JANUARY 10th

ABRAHAM THE FRIEND   *Reading: Genesis 18. 16–33.*

Abraham needed a friend. This we can understand for we all have the same need. What is so surprising is to find that God also desired to have a friend, and found one in Abraham. God was Abraham's Friend. That was wonderful but understandable for He is our Friend too. What is so extraordinary is that Abraham could be God's friend (Isaiah 41.8). He showed himself to be so in the matter of Lot and Sodom. His argument showed no lack of respect, but was calculated to bring out the greatness of his great Friend's character. This is what a true friend does; he draws the best out of us, just as a false friend draws out the worst. Abraham was a good friend to Lot, but even more he was a loyal friend to God. This is surely the pinnacle of human attainment.

JANUARY 11th

ABRAHAM THE WORSHIPPER *Reading: Genesis 22. 1–19.*

God gave Isaac to Abraham by a miracle. He then asked Abraham to sacrifice this precious son of his, even though it seemed essential for the fulfilment of the divine promise that Isaac should live. The birth of Isaac had been almost a resurrection, for he had come when natural capacities had virtually died. Now if Isaac were to be placed on the altar it seemed that a literal resurrection would be needed. Abraham found that he could trust God for this: if Isaac were truly God's gift to him then he did not have to scheme or struggle to retain him, but only to let him go, and rely on God's faithfulness. This is a basic principle for all men and women who have a divine gift.

JANUARY 12th

ABSALOM *Reading: 2 Samuel 18. 24–33.*

If anyone doubts the wisdom of God's original decree of monogamy (the same which has now become a sacred rule of Christianity), he had better read the story of David's unhappy family life, and especially the tragic story of Absalom. Here was a lad full of character and of promise, handsome in his person and winsome in his manners, but whose background was so complicated and insecure that it is no wonder he became the pioneer and prince of all delinquent sons. What chance had he to grow up normally in the pitiful travesty of family life which was all that he knew of home? David wept over him because he knew that Absalom was more to be pitied than blamed. It was too late to weep for him. Is it too late for us to cry to God for a recovery of decent home life?

JANUARY 13th

ACHAN   *Reading:* Joshua 7. 19–26.

Achan was not quarrelsome. He was a quiet member of the community who had no thought of being a trouble-maker. Of course he knew that he was doing wrong in looting from the Jericho ruins, but as he dug his hole in the tent and buried the stolen articles he had no thought of making trouble for others. So far as he was concerned it was his own business. Nevertheless no man lives in isolation; whether he wishes it or not his behaviour is bound to affect others. Thirty-six Israelitish soldiers lost their lives unnecessarily at Ai because of what lay hidden in Achan's tent. In the end his whole family shared in his tragic end. Before we act impulsively, as Achan did, we should remember that our actions always involve others as well as ourselves.

JANUARY 14th

ACHSAH   *Reading:* Joshua 15. 16–19.

We might not have noticed this little romance of Caleb's daughter if it had not been repeated in the book of Judges. Her bridegroom, Othniel, had plenty of physical courage for he had won his wife by hard fighting. Not all her persuasion, however, could induce him to go back to Caleb and ask for springs of water to irrigate their new property: he lacked the moral courage. Failing to persuade him, Achsah saw that the only thing to do was to dismount and go over to talk to her father for herself. She got what she wanted, and we have the impression that Caleb was pleased to give it to her. He could appreciate moral courage as well as physical as he himself had both. Perhaps he felt that this marriage of the two gave good promise for the future.

JANUARY 15th

ADAH   *Reading: Genesis 4. 19–21.*

Adah was the mother of orchestral music. By his double marriage her forceful husband initiated both science and art. Zillah's son was the originator of technology, while Adah's second son, Jubal, invented musical instruments, both strings and wind. From these simple beginnings there has emerged such a plethora of music-making that some may be tempted to doubt the value of Adah's gift to the world; yet a large place is given in the Bible to the use of musical instruments. Prophets were helped to speak, soldiers to fight, and sufferers to find relief because of the use of variations and developments of Jubal's harps and pipes. Even the new song of heaven is to have an orchestral accompaniment (Revelation 14. 2).

JANUARY 16th

ADAM   *Reading: Genesis 1. 26–31.*

Almost every reference to Adam in the New Testament shows him in a bad light. Yet at his beginning the progenitor of our race was full of promise, a fore-shadowing of Christ Himself. Adam was a noble man, made in the image of God. He was a regal man, entrusted with the subduing of God's creation to his will. He was a highly intelligent man, capable of inventing names for all the rest of creation. He was a distinguished man, clothed with a divine aura which only disappeared when he sinned, leaving him naked and ashamed. In fact he was such a wonderful being that his Creator considered him to be "very good". One thing, however, he lacked, and that was faith. He could not trust his God. Such a lack is bound to lead to tragedy.

JANUARY 17th

ADONI-BEZEK   *Reading: Judges 1. 1–7.*

This was not his name but his title, for he was a lord—a war lord! He had invented a fiendish way of humiliating the kings whom he defeated in battle. He had their big toes and their thumbs amputated so that they could neither walk nor grasp any object. These mutilations made them conspicuous and held them captive as effectively as any prison, rendering escape impossible. They grovelled around on the floor under his table and like animals snapped up any bits of food which were thrown down to them. When the total number of these unfortunates reached seventy, retribution came to him. His own thumbs and great toes were cut off. So often men reap what they sow, even in this life.

JANUARY 18th

ADONIJAH   *Reading: 1 Kings 1. 5–13.*

Apparently Adonijah was the eldest surviving son of David, but like his brother Absalom he had been spoiled by his indulgent father and was quite unfitted to reign. We presume that Solomon's upbringing had been more disciplined since it was he who pointed out the value of loving correction (Hebrews 12. 5–6). From the first he had been destined for the throne and so had been strictly disciplined, in contrast with these half-brothers of his who had always been allowed to have their own way. At times he probably envied them, as we are inclined to envy others their easier life. But he lived to see that an unchastened Adonijah could never inherit the kingdom; hence his message to all who are called to inherit God's kingdom, that they should not despise His discipline of love.

JANUARY 19th

AGABUS   *Reading: Acts 21. 7–14.*

It was a burdened Agabus who waved goodbye to Paul and his party as they left Philip's house for their journey to Jerusalem. Either the Lord had abandoned him after fourteen years of successful prophesying (Acts 11. 28) or else he was still a true prophet and the beloved Paul was walking into a trap. Well, at least he could still pray. Paul would not listen to him, but God would. So he and the other sorrowing believers claimed that the will of God should triumph in spite of all. About two weeks afterwards the news went round that Paul was back again in Caesarea and was safe! It was true that he was a prisoner, but he was alive and well. So Agabus's bewilderment gave place to praise. His prophesying had failed but his prayer had succeeded. When our warnings fall on deaf ears we too can pray.

JANUARY 20th

AGUR   *Reading: Proverbs 30. 1–9.*

It is good for a man to have a modest opinion of himself, but perhaps Agur went too far, especially in the lack of self-confidence shown in his earnest request for a life of "safety first". On the surface his may sound a pious prayer, never to be too rich or too poor but just to have enough, yet it may well represent a flight from responsibility. How much more adventurous—yes, and more spiritual—was Paul's declaration that by God's grace he knew both how to be poor and how to be rich. We can prove the Lord in poverty, if that is His choice for us. We can also prove Him in affluence if we exercise a wise stewardship. We may be able to work hard and earn good money and then use it for His kingdom. Not self first, but not safety first either!

JANUARY 21st

AHAB   *Reading: 1 Kings 18. 41–46.*

Ahab married in defiance of the known will of God. The consequences of such a marriage are likely to be tragic. God, however, still gave him one supreme opportunity of recovering from his disastrous union when he drove down to Jezreel with the dark rain clouds all around him. God had spoken to him that day both by the obvious futility of his wife's Sidonian religion and by the fire which fell from heaven. Shaken, convinced, nearly converted, he went home to his idolatrous wife to put things right. But Jezebel had her way still and he proved, as many since have done, that when two people are unequally yoked together it is usually the unspiritual partner who decides their course. No wonder Elijah nearly broke his heart with disappointment.

JANUARY 22nd

AHASUERUS   *Reading: Esther 6. 1–10.*

Ahasuerus is a royal title; the true name of this man was Xerxes; history confirms that he was a capricious, headstrong and violent man. To us he is an outstanding example of how God can turn a sleepless night to profit, so that it serves His purposes and answers His people's prayers. The marvel of such occurrences is their timing. Some may crave for sensational happenings to prove the wisdom and power of God, but to the devout believer the greatest miracles are sometimes simple happenings of life which are yet perfectly timed to realise the divine end. One night earlier or one night later and it would have been meaningless, but it was "that night". God's timings are miraculously perfect.

JANUARY 23rd

AHAZ   *Reading: 2 Kings 16. 7–17.*

Ahaz was a worldly wise planner who despised a simple believer like Isaiah. He would not think of asking God for a sign! After all, such an action might put him under an obligation. Not that he was irreligious. Look at the beautiful Damascene altar which he had ordered to be specially made. Anyhow he did not believe in signs but in hard money. He had no patience with Isaiah's repeated urge to trust the Lord, preferring his own plan of buying help from the influential world power of his day. His plan seemed to work at the time, but when they came to count the cost at the end of his reign they found that he had greatly impoverished God's house. Worldly wisdom in the work of God always results in spiritual poverty.

JANUARY 24th

AHIJAH   *Reading: 1 Kings 14. 1–10.*

When Isaac was blind through old age he was sadly deceived as to the identity of his own son. When the prophet Ahijah was in the same state of physical decay he had no difficulty in penetrating the disguise of Jeroboam's wife, a woman whom he hardly knew. The reason was that he did not wait to taste the loaves and cakes and honey which she brought him. In this he differed very much from Isaac who made the whole interview with his son to centre upon the dish of venison which his soul loved. The truth is that when we have personal interests we lose our capacity to discern spiritual things. That is why God told Moses, "Thou shalt take no gift: for the gift blindeth the seeing, and perverteth the words of the righteous" (Exodus 23.8).

JANUARY 25th

AHITHOPHEL *Reading: 2 Samuel 17. 14–23.*

Ahithophel was a gambler, a calculating gambler who had unbounded confidence in his own judgment. To him loyalty meant nothing: personal gain everything. He readily transferred his allegiance from David to Absalom for the sake of this gain. His advice was excellent—it always was—but it was rejected, and he was shrewd enough to know that its rejection could bring nothing but disaster to Absalom's cause. He had gambled and lost, so he went straight home and committed a gambler's suicide. With all his sagacity Ahithophel had lacked that fear of the Lord which is the beginning of true wisdom, and so he had gambled not against human odds but against God. Such gamblers always lose.

JANUARY 26th

AMAZIAH *Reading: 2 Chronicles 25. 1–9.*

Obedience is often costly. Amaziah was willing to obey the man of God in giving up his unholy alliance with the Northern Kingdom, but he could not face the loss of the one hundred talents which he had already paid them for their help. This constituted no difficulty at all to the prophet, whose immediate response was one of complete confidence in God's ability not only to make good the sum but to give the king much more. Amaziah accepted this assurance and proved it to be quite true. We can afford to forget the mistakes and faults of Amaziah if we remember this lesson which he has left for us, namely that we may count on the faithfulness of God to give us much more than we stand to lose if we obey Him without counting the cost.

JANUARY 27th

AMOS   *Reading: Amos 7. 10–17.*

Unlike many other prophets Amos was neither a student nor a priest, but a working man who eked out an inadequate livelihood as herdman by further humble employment as a dresser of sycamore trees. It was God who took him away from this work and sent him to the unfriendly people of the Northern Kingdom. Amaziah, himself a professional, thought that Amos only prophesied to earn a living, and so suggested that he should get a job in Judah where his type of ministry would go down better. He little knew what kind of man he was addressing. God's true servants do not allow themselves to be hired by men. They do not take up their work as a means of livelihood but as the result of a divine urge. Amos was God sent.

JANUARY 28th

AMRAM   *Reading: Exodus 2. 1–10.*

What a man this husband of Jochabed must have been! It would be enough for most people to have one genius in the family. Amram was father to three. How could these unknown parents, living in slavery, produce such gifted children as Miriam, Aaron and Moses? Well, some parents have clever children and some do not. There is little that they can do about it. When it comes to spiritual qualities, however, there is something that they can do. At a time when many Israelites were dispirited and without faith, Amram and his wife brought up their children to know the value of prayer and praise. These lessons they never forgot. We cannot force our children to have faith, but we can inspire them by our example.

JANUARY 29th

ANANIAS OF JERUSALEM   *Reading: Acts 5. 1–11.*

When Philetus and his companions turned from the truth and worked destruction on other people's faith Paul could only pray about it (2 Timothy 2.17). When Diotrophes slandered John he was threatened by a visit from the aged apostle. When, however, Ananias and his wife lied to Peter they were met by sudden death. Why was this? Certainly not because Peter had greater power than Paul or John. The spirits of Ananias and Sapphira may have been saved even though their bodies died, and probably their death was meant to illustrate for all the rest of the dispensation that it is impossible to deceive the Holy Spirit. Many a modern Ananias experiences death and darkness in the soul though his body lives on.

JANUARY 30th

ANANIAS OF DAMASCUS   *Reading: Acts 9. 10–22.*

In your past have you ever had a moment when you almost missed doing something important? Every time you think back to that moment do you breathe a sigh of gratitude that the Lord saved you from missing that opportunity which seemed insignificant then but proved to be so vital? If so you will know what Ananias must often have felt when he heard of the marvellous ministry of Paul and remembered that morning in Damascus when the Lord prompted him to visit the hated Saul of Tarsus and he almost refused to go. He really did not feel it possible to go to the street called Straight and call that evil man his "brother". Of course he did not then know of Saul's desperate need. "Thank God," Ananias must often have murmured, "Thank God that I did not fail him at that historic moment of crisis."

JANUARY 31st

ANANIAS THE HIGH PRIEST   *Reading: Acts 23. 1-5.*

Like his Lord, Paul was struck across the face in the presence of
the high priest. Jesus, the perfect Man, was unprovoked and
merely rebuked His assailant in quiet dignity (John 18. 23).
Paul was a great saint, but he was by no means perfect, and
he could not repress an angry retort at the evident injustice.
He made some kind of apology but his further comment was
probably more sarcastic than regretful. Yet divine prophecy
seems to have come through his outburst, for soon Ananias was
dismissed from his office by the authorities and he was later
brutally murdered in the streets of Jerusalem. Prophecy is
God's prerogative. He can make known His purposes by any
means which He chooses; if necessary even through ill-
considered words.

FEBRUARY 1st

ANDREW   *Reading: John 1. 35-42.*

Andrew's special virtue seems to have been that of becoming
a living link between others and the Saviour. He first intro-
duced his own brother, Simon Peter, to Christ, and leaves us
all indebted to him for this initiative. He it was who found
the lad with the five barley loaves and the two fishes and took
him to the Lord (John 6. 8, 9) and it was also he who helped
to deal with the Greeks who wanted to see Jesus (John 12. 21,
22). It is surely significant that all these actions of Andrew's
were not recorded until he and the other apostles except
John had left this earth. So often God does not like to give His
servants publicity in this life, but judges it best for us to wait
and receive our commendation in eternity.

FEBRUARY 2nd

ANNA   *Reading: Luke 2. 33–38.*

When Moses blessed the tribe of Asher he added the promise,
"As thy days, so shall thy strength be" (Deuteronomy 33. 25).
Anna was a true daughter of Asher. Instead of moping over
her early widowhood she was forward-looking and made
every day—and every night also—a fresh occasion for proving
how God gives strength just as it is needed. For her the
greatest day of all came when she was quite old, but she was
equal to it, alert in her recognition of the Saviour and energetic
in the inspiration she gave to those around her. Some people
allow their lack of strength to decide the course of the day:
as their strength is so is their day. Anna was not of this
number but as a spiritual child of Asher she entered each day
with God, counting wholly on Him.

FEBRUARY 3rd

ANNAS   *Reading: Acts 4. 6–18.*

Historically Annas had been deposed from the high priesthood
long before this, yet he was the effective power still, and had
been while his sons and son-in-law, Caiaphas, held the office.
Annas could not ignore the evident spiritual effectiveness of
the apostles and had to admit that a notable miracle had
occurred, but he spurned this last offer of blessing through
Christ. Other considerations weighed more with him, all of
them worldly or selfish, with the result that he committed the
unpardonable sin of finally closing his conscience to the light
of God's truth. This was the sin against the Holy Ghost, and
for that there is no forgiveness—not even for a "high priest"!

FEBRUARY 4th

ANTIPAS   *Reading: Revelation 2. 12–17.*

When Athanasius, in his stand for the deity of Christ, was informed that the whole world was against him he replied with simple dignity, "Then I am against the whole world." Since the name of Antipas can mean "against all", it appears that this man had the same kind of courageous faith. God had honoured him and the believers at Pergamum by locating them in a place which could only be described as Satan's headquarters. We may feel that something like this has happened to us. Why does God expose His servants in this way? He does it because He knows that Christ who is "the Faithful Witness" can give grace to every Antipas to be a faithful witness also. This grace is called "the hidden manna" and is available to sustain and fortify every tried servant of God.

FEBRUARY 5th

APOLLOS   *Reading: Acts 18. 24–28.*

It was no wonder that Apollos became a great teacher, for he himself was willing to sit humbly in the tent-maker's home and be taught. His name became a byword among the churches. "You must hear Apollos," the believers would say to one another; "there is not another preacher like him." This was especially so at Corinth where a whole group was infatuated with him and despised Paul. Naturally Paul's friends rallied to the defence of their beloved apostle so that there was an unhappy rivalry in the church. Horrified, Paul got in touch with Apollos at once and strongly urged him to return to Corinth while he himself would stay away. Apollos however refused. It was not at all his will nor was it the will of God that any glory should be given to the name of Apollos.

FEBRUARY 6th

AQUILA   *Reading: Acts 18. 1–3.*

Anti-semitism was already operative in the first century. Aquila and his wife were its victims. Nevertheless God made their unjust treatment to turn out for blessing. Cruelly expelled from their business, the Jewish couple had to begin all over again in Corinth. When they needed an extra worker who should apply but the apostle Paul? As the three worked they talked, with the result that soon Aquila and Priscilla were rejoicing in their new-found Saviour. Apollos later found Christ in their home and later "all the churches of the Gentiles" became indebted to them (Romans 16.4). There is something Satanic about anti-semitism. It is as unreasonable as it is cruel. God, however, can use even the workings of the devil to bring blessing to men.

FEBRUARY 7th

ARCHIPPUS   *Reading: Colossians 4. 17.*

Archippus was perhaps a "one talent" man. We have no knowledge of what his gift was but we do know that it is the peril of such men that they should hide their one talent and bury it, instead of keeping it in circulation. Paul was such an outstanding figure that the very demands made upon him kept him active in the use of his ten talents. Timothy, the five talent man, must also have been inspired to soldier on by his position. Archippus, however, could easily have relapsed into inactivity if he had not received this sharp reminder from Paul that he must not slack off at all. Even if he only had one talent it had been entrusted to him not by Paul but by the Lord whom he loved and he must take great care to make full use of it.

FEBRUARY 8th

ARTAXERXES *Reading: Ezra 7. 11–26.*

This Persian monarch was called Longimanus, that is "Long Handed". Probably the title referred to the extent of his dominion, but for Ezra and his friends it was an open hand as well as a long one which wrote their letter of commendation. The supplies which Ezra could dispose of were specified in a lavish way, with the finishing touch of generosity "and salt without prescribing how much." Salt was, and is, a vital necessity of life. It was also an essential for the Israelites' sacrifices. So here is the reminder that when God sends His servants on a mission, as He sent Ezra, the royal edict is issued from heaven that there should always be adequate supplies for life and worship. God's "long-handed" grace is without limit.

FEBRUARY 9th

ASA *Reading: 2 Chronicles 16. 7–14.*

Asa was a king who for many years stood before the Lord. He stood for purity of worship and for the safety of Judah's cities. He stood in the face of the great Ethiopian army and God gave him victory. He stood to listen to the prophet Azariah's wise advice and he showed great courage in his stand. He stood so nobly that he became a rallying point for other tribes who were encouraged by his example. He stood amid a sound of trumpets to make a covenant of faithfulness to God. He even stood against his own mother and deposed her. How strange, then, that this should be the king to succumb finally to a disease of the feet. His story is a graphic reminder of the warning, "Let him that thinketh he standeth take heed lest he fall" (1 Corinthians 10. 12).

FEBRUARY 10th

ASAHEL   *Reading: 2 Samuel 2. 18–24.*

Asahel was an outstandingly fast runner, but to the warrior speed is not everything. He could outrun Abner but he was no match for him in the actual conflict, and so he met with disaster. Asahel ran so fast that he left behind his two older and stronger brothers whom he so much needed. He tried to manage the affair without their help, but it was too much for him alone and by the time that his brothers arrived he had received the mortal blow. He might have avoided this tragedy if he had only waited for his brothers and for the strength and protection which always comes from fellowship. The same truth is valid in the matter of spiritual activities. Eagerness and quickness are very useful but they need to be balanced by experience. We must learn to wait for our brothers.

FEBRUARY 11th

ASAPH   *Reading: 1 Chronicles 25. 1–3.*

Asaph finally reached the high position of master of the king's music. He had twelve psalms attributed to his name. Yet he seems to have begun his career as a cymbal player (1 Chronicles 15. 19). Cymbals are a very humble accompaniment to music but they are not nearly so easy to play as may appear. It is notable that they have a double mention in the last psalm in the book and that there they are given an honoured place in the offering of praise to the Lord. The truth is that a cymbalist must have sustained strength: other instrumentalists have their occasional bursts of prominence and their bars of rest but the cymbal player must not let up. This is the basis of all true praise, the ability to keep steadily on without pause and without variation.

FEBRUARY 12th

ATHALIAH   *Reading: 2 Kings 11. 1–4.*

Six is the number of man, so it is not surprising that Athaliah
reigned for six years. This murderous daughter of Jezebel was
a striking example of how bad a human being can become.
The six years, however, had an end and relief came in the
seventh. It was a divine intervention but it was made possible
by Jehoida and his godly wife who worked and prayed in the
dark days of satanic supremacy, never deviating from their
purpose of seeing God's rightful king placed on the throne.
Antichrist's number will be six hundred and sixty six, for he
will be the full expression of how bad a man can be. But the
seventh trumpet will sound and God's true King will come to
reign for ever and ever. Meanwhile there is need for men and
women who will keep the faith and love His appearing.

FEBRUARY 13th

AUGUSTUS   *Reading: Luke 2. 1–7.*

Augustus began as a member of the ruling triumvirate of
Rome but was finally left as sole ruler and was the first of the
Caesars to be called Emperor. He neither knew nor cared
about Micah's prophecy concerning Bethlehem, but his was
the decree which ensured that Joseph and Mary should have
to leave their Galilee home and journey to that town, arriving
just in time for the birth of the infant Jesus. Augustus made
history in all parts of the world, but all unconsciously his most
significant contribution to history was when he signed the
decree for his census. Why should we ever doubt the over-
ruling wisdom of our wonderful God? Augustus, there is One
more august than you, and even through you He can work all
things to do His will and fulfil His Word.

FEBRUARY 14th

AZARIAH *Reading: Daniel 3. 14–18.*

The Apocrypha gives us many verses of praise which were reputedly sung by the three Hebrews as they strolled to and fro in the white hot furnace. Naturally the Babylonish names are not used, so that the third member of the group is called by his true name, Azariah. According to the Apocryphal verses the three radiant believers went through a long list of God's created works before they came to themselves, appealing to each in turn to praise and magnify the Lord. The gem in this collection is found in the words, "O ye Fire and Heat, bless ye the Lord: praise Him and magnify Him for ever." The man who can voice such a song when he is actually in the fire is surely unconquerable.

FEBRUARY 15th

BALAAM *Reading: Numbers 22. 15–35.*

Balaam was an inspiring preacher, endued with the Spirit. He was a gifted prophet, and he knew how to pray. He even had longings for heaven after death. Yet he missed God's way and God's blessing. He warns us to beware of outward gifts if there is no inward grace, to beware of keeping on praying about the Lord's will after He has already made it plain, to beware of persisting in ways of self-will when even an ass can tell us that we are being foolish, and to beware of getting angry with the "ass" who does so warn us. We must beware of talking much about God's glory in public and following self-interest in private. These are the marks of those who are in danger of falling into the error of Balaam—and what a tragic error it proved to be!

FEBRUARY 16th

BALAK   *Reading: Numbers 23. 13–23.*

Balak deliberately took the medium, Balaam, to a place where he could only see a fringe of the camp, feeling that if he could attack the nation in isolated groups he might overthrow it. What he did not realise, however, was that God's people dwelt as one (24. 2) and as such were invincible. Balaam might focus his vision on a few tents but God made him see them as part of a united and ordered people under divine government, and in view of this he was forced to inform Balak that curses only had the opposite effect, resulting in blessings. Christians need not fear satanic assaults if they abide together under the Headship of Christ. God can still turn the curse into a blessing.

FEBRUARY 17th

BARAK   *Reading: Judges 4. 6–15.*

Barak would have been the first to deny that any credit should be given him for the victory. He was no hero. In fact he seems to have been a character with little personal drive who had to lean on a woman at every stage. Many of us will have fellow feelings with him. We, too, are bad starters, full of doubts and fears, always needing someone to lean on. "What can we do for the Lord?" we ask. "How can our little faith make any difference?" Let us take courage from Barak. His little faith was enough to get heaven moving—the stars in their courses fought against Sisera (Judges 5. 20). We need not wait until our faith and confidence grow greater but use the little faith that we have. Perhaps that is true heroism.

FEBRUARY 18th

BARNABAS   *Reading: Acts 11. 19–26.*

In a book full of fine Spirit-filled men it may be surprising to find only this one called "good". Perhaps he was good because he was quick to appreciate good in others. When the apostles would not trust Saul of Tarsus it was Barnabas who sponsored him to them. When he was sent to Antioch he could doubtless have found much to criticise if he had looked for it, since the church was immature and leaderless. Instead he looked for good things, found them and was glad to do so. When Mark asked to be given a second chance and Paul said "No", Barnabas differed because he could look beyond Mark's failure and see some good in him. Barnabas was right on each of these occasions. It is surely good to look for good in others and to rejoice when it is found.

FEBRUARY 19th

BARABBAS   *Reading: Matthew 27. 15–26.*

To any story teller with an eye for the dramatic, Barabbas provides the perfect illustration of salvation. As Christ was being arrested he already lay under sentence of death with his two companions. The very cross must have been all ready for his execution. The next morning his prison door was opened and he was released, and that without any effort of his. Because of Pilate's decision he was completely freed from the law's condemnation and from its fierce penalty, while the Son of God took his place and was hanged on his cross. It is a striking illustration of substitution, yet the Scriptures imply that it did him no lasting good. The Bible is no story book but tells of facts, and the sad fact is that the power of the Cross is only for the believer.

FEBRUARY 20th

BARSABBAS   *Reading: Acts 1. 15–26.*

At John the Baptist's call Joseph Barsabbas left all to follow the Lamb, but he was given no place among the Twelve. Undeterred and unoffended he never forsook the group, but was always at hand. The Lord Jesus gave him no special attention and did not even refer to him and Matthias as possible successors to Judas. Many more may have started with the original disciples, but by the time of the pre-Pentecostal prayer meetings the short list of possible candidates for apostleship was reduced to two. Then after more prayer the eleven cast the lot to decide who should occupy the vacant post. Matthias was chosen and so Barsabbas had his final disappointment. Seemingly he did not take offence, but stayed on and served with the rank and file. We need more of this type of man in our churches today.

FEBRUARY 21st

BARTIMAEUS   *Reading: Mark 10. 46–52.*

Had Bartimaeus not been made a beggar by his blindness he might never have become a follower of Jesus. Many people with sight looked at Jesus without any lasting result. They were looking at Him when they told Bartimaeus to keep quiet. If he had possessed good sight and had a good job he might have remained as indifferent as they. But he was in trouble. He was in so much trouble that nobody could silence him. He was so desperate that when asked about his need he did not waste words (as we often do) but made his prayer direct. The answer was just as direct. He was given his sight. So his blindness and his poverty proved to be blessings, for they brought Christ into his life and made him ready to receive divine riches. In this same way God is ready to turn men's calamities and handicaps into blessings—if they will let Him.

FEBRUARY 22nd

BARUCH   *Reading: Jeremiah 45.*

Even the most courageous man has his moments of doubt and depression. In prison or out of it, Baruch had never failed Jeremiah; he had even risked his life to serve him. One day, however, he gave way to self-pity in the presence of his great colleague, who himself had sometimes felt and spoken in just the same way. Jeremiah must have seemed very unsympathetic as he put his finger on Baruch's weak spot. Could not the prophet have said something softer and more soothing? No, we are not saved from self-pity by smooth words; they only make us more sorry for ourselves. Jeremiah administered the same shock treatment which God had given him in his depression (12. 5). It hurt but it worked. It uncovered the hidden self-seeking which was the cause of the trouble and which is usually the cause of self-pity. God's servants must not expect to live soft.

FEBRUARY 23rd

BARZILLAI   *Reading: 2 Samuel 19. 31–40.*

In fleeing from the rebellious Absalom, David went east over Jordan. His followers and he were weary and hungry but they were relieved by the kind generosity of a local landowner named Barzillai. Others were afraid to help but he was one of the few who remained true. The tide turned. Absalom was defeated. When David's exile was over he wished to honour Barzillai as his own guest in Jerusalem. The old man declined the honour, being glad enough to return home with the quiet satisfaction which comes to all loyal hearts who have done their duty without hope of reward. His wishes were respected, but still the honour of a perpetual place at the king's table was assured to the sons who bore his name (1 Kings 2. 7). God's king is determined that the men who have been true to him in his rejection shall have a permanent place with him in his exaltation.

FEBRUARY 24th

BATHSHEBA   *Reading: 2 Samuel 11. 1–15.*

Uriah, Bathsheba's husband, was a noble character. Perhaps she would have been true to him if anyone less than the king had flattered her with his attentions. It was by flattery, too, that Adonijah got her help concerning Abishag, nearly causing disaster to her son, Solomon. She gives the impression that she was one of those people who can be too easily persuaded by soft words. When such folk are flattered they do not know how to say "No". God did not blame Bathsheba for the adultery; He blamed David for that. Nor did He blame her for Uriah's death to which she was probably not even party. But her "one small petition" to Solomon (1 Kings 2. 20) was very foolish and should never have been made. We do well to view all flattery with suspicion.

FEBRUARY 25th

BELSHAZZAR   *Reading: Daniel 5. 17–31.*

Belshazzar did what many others still do; he applauded God's messenger but then ignored God's message. In this way he failed to know the deliverance which he might have had. For while it was inevitable that Darius should complete his capture of the kingom, Belshazzar himself need not have died. In fact Babylon was captured without a struggle, the only fatality in the transfer of power being this foolish ruler: he was more concerned for the brilliant success of his Banquet of a Thousand Guests than for his own soul's well-being. The writing on the wall was a timely warning. Who knows what mercy he might have found if he had treated this last warning seriously! It would have been better to have done that than to heap honours on Daniel, the interpreter.

FEBRUARY 26th

BENAIAH *Reading: 2 Samuel 23. 20–23.*

Benaiah was a man who thrived on adversity. It was not enough for him to battle with lion-like men, he could not be satisfied with anything less than conflict with a real lion. To him it gave just the opportunity that he wanted to prove the value of living faith in a living God. Most men would have waited for a better arena than a pit. From a pit there could be no flight, for once he was in it with the lion he had to see the thing through. And all this on a snowy day! A snowstorm would have provided any ordinary man with an excellent excuse for postponing the confrontation. Benaiah was not looking for excuses. He was not prepared to wait for fairer weather. The mounting difficulties merely acted as spurs to faith and he found honour—as we may find it—by facing difficulties and triumphing over adversities.

FEBRUARY 27th

BEN-HADAD *Reading: 1 Kings 20. 23–28.*

Ben-hadad's Syrian advisers made a very common mistake when they thought that God could only help His people when they were in the hills. Even believers fall into this same error, rejoicing at the Lord's nearness on mountain-top occasions but falling into doubt and gloom when life's conflicts take them down into some deep valley. God gladly took up Ben-hadad's challenge and proved His sufficiency in the valley also. His harassed people found that He gave them a wonderful victory and He also gave the lie to unbelief. Valley experiences certainly test us, but they present no problem to God. If anything it is in the deep places that He is best able to show us His supernatural power, and to demonstrate to the Ben-hadads of this world how wonderful He is.

FEBRUARY 28th

BENJAMIN   *Reading: Genesis 43. 26–34.*

Benjamin proved to be the peacemaker in his divided family. They were all drawn together not so much by what he said or by what he did but simply by his presence. When the ten sons of Jacob went down to Egypt to buy corn they were left in no doubt that they must not return without Benjamin. Only under the direst necessity would his father finally let him go. We may find it difficult to understand Joseph's apparent harshness with his brothers, but it is very clear that he felt great affection for the youngest of the family. From their side the other brothers found unity in their genuine desire to protect Benjamin for their old father's sake. So ultimately Benjamin brought the whole family together just by being himself. In our day there is a real need for peacemakers who can unite the divided family of God's people.

FEBRUARY 29th

BEZALEL   *Reading: Exodus 35. 30–35.*

The idea that the fulness of the Spirit is necessarily intended to make preachers of us all is erroneous. Bezalel was an artisan, but he was filled with the Spirit in order to use his hands in the service of God. He was as much a worker for God as any preacher, with a task of fundamental importance requiring care as well as skill. Some Christians are irked at having to devote their training and abilities to merely secular jobs, chafing under a desire to be freed for what they call "full-time service". Bezalel's example reminds us that one of the secrets of the Spirit's fulness is to do all our daily work thoroughly and to do it for the glory of God (Colossians 3. 23). We are all called into "full-time service" and are not permitted to make a distinction between the sacred and the secular.

MARCH 1st

BOAZ   *Reading: Ruth 3. 1–13.*

When Solomon set up his two brass columns in the Temple porch he called one of them Boaz—"In him is strength" (1 Kings 7. 21). Ruth would have agreed. To her Boaz was the embodiment of all that is upright and reliable; he was a pillar of strength. Disqualified by birth, weakened by widowhood and brought low by poverty, Ruth had no one to lean on when first she came to Bethlehem. It was there that she met the family redeemer who completely transformed her life. This is a love story, and its simple purity stands in great contrast to the contemporary history of the book of Judges. Our world, like hers, is full of violence and evil and our condition as needy as hers. For us, too, there is a Redeemer from Bethlehem who is fully qualified and very ready to help us. In Him is strength!

MARCH 2nd

CAIN   *Reading: Genesis 4. 1–15.*

Why did Cain become an outcast? Not only because of his envy of Abel, for most of us have been guilty of that sin. Not only because he killed his brother, for our consciences accuse us of having had murderous thoughts, even if we have not put them into effect. No, Cain's supreme sin was that he tried to hide his sin. Had he waited by his brother's corpse, until God came to him, humbly confessing his foul deed, he would certainly have found mercy. He could have taken God to the shallow grave and admitted his shameful action, but instead he only countered God's question with surly impenitence. He felt no awe at God's presence and no regret for his sin, but only a mean fear that someone might do to him what he had done to his unsuspecting brother. There can never be a place in the paradise of God for that kind of man.

MARCH 3rd

CAIAPHAS *Reading: John 11. 49–53.*

Although there had been attempts to assassinate the Lord
Jesus before, the actual decision to plot His death was made in
this Council of the Jewish leaders. Caiaphas, the corrupt High
Priest, prided himself on being the author of the plan and even
justified it with a hypocritical excuse that it was to save the
nation. John explains to us, however, that all unintentionally
Caiaphas was being used as the voice of divine prophecy. In
spite of his unholy character something came through him of
the Urim and Thummim (Lights and Perfections) by which
the will of God had been made known. The initiative was not
with Caiaphas; it was with God. By divine overruling the
murder was to be made a means of reconciling redeemed men
to God and to one another. God is never on the defensive.
Poor, conceited Caiaphas was only a tool after all.

MARCH 4th

CANDACE *Reading: Acts 8. 27–35.*

When Candace's treasurer returned from his visit to Jerusalem
he took her back something infinitely more precious than all
her wealth, that is the Gospel of God's love in Jesus Christ.
We know nothing of her personally, though secular historians
confirm that there was a succession of Nubian queens who used
the title of Candace. Nor do we know anything of the impact
on her kingdom of the arrival of this high official who was so
overflowing with the joy of salvation. A man who was so
much in earnest that he could invite a travel-stained stranger
to sit with him in his chariot and who was so soundly converted that he could plead to be given the first opportunity of
confessing Christ in baptism, even in front of his own servants,
was hardly likely to maintain silence about his new-found
faith when he returned to court duties at home.

MARCH 5th

CALEB   *Reading: Joshua 14. 6–14.*

Caleb is a great example of a faith which never gives up. When the ten spies turned back in unbelief he stood firm with a different spirit. That was a great achievement, but still greater was his persevering faith which kept him steadfastly counting on God's promise through all the wasted years. He could not reverse God's rejection of his own generation, nor could he disassociate himself from the others and enter the Promised Land alone. No, he had to take his place among his fellow Israelites through the forty years of wilderness frustration and yet to be different from them in spirit. Unbelief and impatience are very contagious, but Caleb escaped them by keeping his heart set on God. Such a man not only survives himself but becomes a living link between a hopeless breakdown and a new generation which can possess the inheritance for God.

MARCH 6th

CEPHAS   *Reading: John 1. 35–42.*

This name is more familiar to us in its Greek form, Peter, but it seems that Cephas was the name more generally used among the early believers. When Christ first gave him the name it was not a recognition of his merits but a promise and a prophecy. Simon was not a rock but God intended to make him one. When God first calls us He also has a name, a purpose, for our lives. We are not to imagine that because we are given a name we automatically become what we should be. Nor must we vainly think that we can change ourselves by our own efforts. Like Cephas it may be possible that the prophecy can only be fulfilled after we have discovered how hopeless we really are. After that dark night of failure came the bright morning of resurrection and then the full day of Pentecost. Simon was still Simon but he was also Cephas, a rock.

MARCH 7th

CHENANIAH   *Reading: 1 Chronicles 15. 22–27.*

Ronald Knox's translation tells us that Chenaniah was "the burden-master". He was stated to be the man responsible for "lifting up", which some translators take to mean the ministry of song. More probably it meant the carrying of the Ark, but once the Temple furniture was permanently settled his office seems to have included the teaching and judging of Israel (1 Chronicles 26. 29). In the wider sweep of public life among God's people he took full responsibility to keep things up to the divine standards. There is much in life today which tends to draw down to lower levels, and even Christians can act as down-drags to their companions. So much greater, then, is the need for those who have Chenaniah's skill to exert their influence for uplift, taking responsibility to keep the spiritual standard high.

MARCH 8th

CHLOE   *Reading: 1 Corinthians 1. 10–17.*

The notable thing about this reference to the house of Chloe is that it was ever openly made by Paul. He had received bad news about the behaviour of the Corinthian Christians, news which he partly believed and felt bound to reprove severely. Normally the name of the informants would have been treated as confidential. Not so with Paul. He would have no secret tale-bearing, no confidential whisperings, but bluntly announced the source of his information to be Chloe's household. This is the only way to avoid malicious gossip. If people have complaints to make about others then let their names be quoted as well as their charges. If they desire to remain anonymous then let us refuse to listen to them. The man of God should never allow himself to become involved in underhand criticisms.

MARCH 9th

CLAUDIUS LYSIAS   *Reading: Acts 23. 23–32.*

When the believers at Caesarea said goodbye to Paul they did
so with many forebodings, and with the tearful prayer that
the will of the Lord might be done. Tearful or not, their
prayer was wonderfully answered and the apostle returned
safely from Jerusalem, even though he came back as a prisoner.
God had answered their prayers, not by means of an angel,
but by a harassed Roman Chiliarch who had paid a lot of
money for his citizenship and had doubtless worked hard to
attain his military command. The assignment given to
Claudius Lysias was to keep the turbulent temple mob in
order; it was a thankless one, and he was determined to take no
chances of harm coming to this free-born Roman citizen. He
therefore arranged for Paul to go back to Caesarea mounted and
with an armed escort. So once again prayer was answered and
truly the will of God was done.

MARCH 10th

CLEOPAS   *Reading: Luke 24. 13–34.*

It may have seemed strange to the other disciples that Cleopas
could have walked and talked with the Lord for so long
without recognising Him. Even when they reached Emmaus
and sat round the table, he and his companion did not realise
who their inspiring Guest could be. Suddenly they recognised
Him. Their Visitor took the loaf in His two hands to break it,
and as He did so they saw the marks which had so far been
hidden from them. There could be no mistaking such ugly
wounds: it was their crucified Lord. His hands had been
crushed and yet they were as strong as ever. His feet had been
pierced and yet He had walked so smoothly along the rough
road. Cleopas and his friend had seen many miracles, but never
one like this. It remains the greatest miracle of all time. They
could not understand the resurrection, but neither could they
doubt it.

MARCH 11th

CORNELIUS   *Reading: Acts 10. 38–40.*

If we want to know what was meant by Peter being given the keys of the kingdom we should study the story of Cornelius. Although he was a devout man, accepted by God, he did not know the way into the kingdom. His prayers could not get him in. His alms could not buy his entrance. Even an angel could not admit him, but could only direct him to God's human steward. So Peter was sent for and after some argument agreed to attend to the matter and go to Caesarea. It was while he was preaching Christ that the Spirit's blessing came. Cornelius and the others were so obviously "in" that it was generally agreed that they should be baptised immediately. The "keys" were a declaration that the kingdom is wide open to all who believe on the Lord Jesus Christ. Cornelius gladly accepted the invitation to enter into the wide open door.

MARCH 12th

CRISPUS   *Reading: Acts 18. 1–10.*

Crispus needed much encouragement; perhaps that is why Paul personally baptised him. God does not make it easy for us when we commit all to Christ. It was certainly not easy for Crispus. For him it meant that he had to leave his synagogue and yet pass it again every time he gathered with the other Christians. He must often have wished that their new meeting place had been in another part of the city. Possibly he had to suffer many insults as he constantly encountered his old Jewish congregation who were almost next door to the house of Justus. They could see that many of the Gentiles with whom he was fraternising were people of low social class (1 Corinthians 1. 26). How much easier it would have been for him if he had stayed away from the meetings and worshipped at home alone! Crispus however did not choose the easy way; he kept true to his baptism.

MARCH 13th

CYRUS   *Reading: Isaiah 45. 1–7.*

"How different the world situation would be," people some-times say, "if only our statesmen were Christians, and prayer-fully sought the will of God." The Bible, however, orders us to pray for rulers even if they are not Christians, for our prayers are directed to the God who uses men to do His will irrespective of whether they know Him or not. Cyrus is a case in point. We may be sure that he was governed by policy rather than by faith when he released the captive Israelites and their sacred vessels, and sent them back to Jerusalem. Whether or not he was influenced by Daniel's counsel he was certainly influenced by his prayers. Although Cyrus did not realise it, the hour had struck for the release of God's captive people, and he was the unwitting fulfiller of divine prophecy. So pagan Cyrus became a servant of the Lord.

MARCH 14th

DAN   *Reading: Genesis 49. 16–18.*

It is not easy to find anything good to say about Dan. Not about his birth, for he was the first of Jacob's servant-girl sons. Not about his maturity, for his old father described him as a treacherous serpent. Not about his succession, for the book of Judges gives the tribe of Dan a bad record. Samson was their great man, but he hardly brought much credit to himself or to his tribe. We look for Dan in vain when we read the final list of God's sealed servants (Revelation 7. 4–8). Was Dan, then, a complete failure? Only eternity will show, for the name means "judgment"—not ours but God's. Our wisdom is to refrain from judging any man and to wait for the verdict to be given by God, the only competent Judge, who knows all the facts. His verdict will be both right and merciful.

MARCH 15th

DANIEL THE YOUTH   *Reading: Daniel 1. 3–17.*

"Daniel purposed in his heart that he would not defile himself
. . . therefore he requested . . . that he might not defile himself." In this he showed a poised balance of firmness and courtesy which is unusual in a youth. Moreover it implies strong
faith in God. When we want to take a stand we often become
fierce and defiant. Our very aggressiveness reveals an inner
uncertainty which is the opposite of true faith. Daniel was so
sure that God rules that he felt no need for the shrill protest of
modern youth. He and his companions ate their simple meals
and pursued their diligent studies with a quiet confidence that
God could not possibly fail them. Nor did He, for the outcome
was that they were "fairer and fatter" and "ten times better"
than those without faith. This is how it should always be.

MARCH 16th

DANIEL THE MAN   *Reading: Daniel 5. 13–31.*

After Daniel's brilliant success as a youth it is a shock to find
him set aside and forgotten in the years which followed. Here
was a tremendous test to the man who knew that he had been
called to rulership. Could he retain his quiet faith even in
obscurity? He could, and he did. Remembered by the Queen
Mother in a moment of crisis, hastily summoned for consultation and offered rich rewards, he replied with a solemn
denunciation of the despicable monarch who called him,
showing himself indifferent to perils or rewards. So it was that
God used the drunken folly of Belshazzar to restore His
chosen servant to his vocation as ruler. All that Daniel had
to do was to wait and to be faithful in the time of crisis;
God took responsibility for his re-instatement.

MARCH 17th

DANIEL THE AGED   *Reading: Daniel 6. 10–23.*

Why was it that this venerable statesman was so hated? He was hated because he prayed. "What!" you may ask. "Is prayer as significant as that?" Yes, it is, when men pray as Daniel did. His prayers were simple, but they were mighty. They reached across the deserts to the ruins of Jerusalem and got to work on restoration. They reached right out of time into the conflict of the unseen world. And they prevailed. It is true that as soon as he had made his evening supplication he was hustled off and thrown to the hungry lions, but at the hour of prayer next morning he was back home on his knees again before the open window. He was, perhaps, a little dishevelled and tired after his unusual night, but he was quietly triumphant. You see, he relied on God. You have to if you really pray!

MARCH 18th

DARIUS   *Reading: Daniel 6. 14–23.*

Poor Darius! He was the ruler of a vast empire and yet he could not get a night's sleep. After a worrying day of anxious deliberations he could only toss to and fro in troubled tension. He might have been thankful for the dawn which came at last, but for the fact that now he had to face the full tragedy resulting from the decree which he had been tricked into signing. Before anybody else was stirring he hurried down to the lions' den and in an anguished voice asked to know the worst. It had not happened. On the contrary, his favourite was still alive and well. For him it had been a night of hell, but then he had no personal experience of reliance on God. For Daniel, however, heaven had been nearer than usual, for both at night and day peace depends on complete trust in the faithfulness of God.

MARCH 19th

DATHAN   *Reading: Numbers 16. 13–35.*

One disaffected person can often arouse bad feelings in many others. Korah, the Levite, started this upset by his jealousy of Aaron. This gave opportunity for the pent-up rebellion of Dathan to be released. His actual complaint was that they were still in the wilderness, but the real cause of grievance was the envy he and his brother felt for Moses. Possibly they based their complaints on the fact that they were members of Reuben, which should have been the senior tribe. It is seldom difficult to find a specious reason to excuse festering jealousy. Times have changed now, so that we no longer witness God's catastrophic judgments, but let us not imagine that God is any more lenient to jealousy. Those who give way to it may seem to survive, but it is still possible to be spiritually "buried alive" because of jealousy and envy.

MARCH 20th

DAVID THE SHEPHERD   *Reading: Psalm 78. 70–72.*

David began as a shepherd. He himself claimed to have learned his first spiritual lessons while defending his father's sheep. As God later reminded him, he was actually called from the sheepfold to receive Samuel's anointing, and what is more he had to resume this occupation more than once before he actually became king. When Nathan wanted to impress him with the enormity of his sin he wisely invented the story of the ewe lamb. It was successful, for David was still a shepherd at heart. His appeal to God for mercy on Israel was based on the argument that the people were unoffending sheep (1 Chronicles 21. 17). It seems that a shepherd heart is a basic requirement for anyone who aspires to serve God among his fellow men.

MARCH 21st

DAVID THE OUTLAW   *Reading: 1 Samuel 26. 13–25.*

For many years after he was anointed king, David was harassed by Saul. He was driven from his wife and home, forced to live in caves and on the mountains, always in danger and sometimes almost in despair. God's ways of preparation are certainly strange. From the lessons of the sheepfold David passed to the lessons of the wilderness. He learned the meaning of fellowship, as he and his men were fused together in the fires of suffering. He learned the need for patience, for he tells us that he "waited patiently for the Lord" and urges us to do the same. He also learned faith in God's promises and distrust of his own efforts. If we can learn faith, patience and practical fellowship in our wilderness experiences we shall be qualifying to reign with Christ.

MARCH 22nd

DAVID THE KING   *Reading: 1 Chronicles 14. 8–17.*

Even as king, David was still prepared to go on learning. He knew that he must learn how to obey commands as well as how to give them. When he finally came to the throne he had passed through long years in which he had been forced to depend on the Lord for day-to-day guidance. Happily he did not abandon this attitude when he became king, for a ruler's first business is to remain teachable and to be willing to get instructions from heaven. We see in this passage how David referred every new circumstance back to God, knowing that he must not decide by his own wisdom, still less merely copy what he had done before. Few things are more menacing to spiritual continuity than the repetition of procedures which have been successful in the past.

MARCH 23rd

DAVID THE WORSHIPPER *Reading: 2 Samuel 7. 1–13.*

David had set his heart on building the house of God. For years his thoughts had been centred on this project and his savings dedicated to its fulfilment. He had prayed about it and had been given a heavenly plan of how it should be constructed. Then came the bombshell! Nathan had to tell him that the work would be done by someone else. David took the disappointment magnificently. He went on preparing the materials, handed over the plans to Solomon, and encouraged him to carry through the task which had been his own life's ambition. This was pure worship, for it proved that he was not at all concerned for himself but only for the glory of God. The man who can cheerfully hand over his work for God to others and still support them in it has become a worshipper in spirit and in truth.

MARCH 24th

DAVID THE SINNER *Reading: Psalm 51. 7–15.*

The sin was secret but the effects were plain to all! David's lips were closed. Goliath had not been able to silence David; Saul had never been able to take away his song; the wilderness, the hardships, even Satan himself had never been able to close David's lips; but what they could not do sin had done. Not that David had been struck dumb. No, he could talk about other things; but what he could not do was speak or sing the praises of God. Sin always has this effect, even when it is not so great as David's was. For this kind of silence there is only one remedy; it is to have the heart cleansed. Once David was again made whiter than snow his lips were opened in praise and the Holy Spirit gave him new release and joy. Sin is the great spiritual silencer.

MARCH 25th

DAVID THE SWEET PSALMIST   *Reading: Psalm 18. 1–16.*

David did not begin with this first verse (2 Samuel 22. 1).
It was when the song was repeated that the words "I love
thee, O Lord . . ." were inserted. And no wonder! For who
could repeat such a story of God's gracious power without
knowing a new upsurge of love in his soul? Perhaps, like us,
David sometimes regretted the coldness of his heart towards
God, feeling that his love was so feeble. Let me recall again, he
seems to say; let me recall again how many troubles I have
been in, and how God has delivered me from them all.
Let me remember the marvellous answers to my prayers and
the undeserved victories given me. Let me not think of my
own nothingness but of His immense greatness! The inevitable
result of such thoughts is to make us exclaim, "I love thee, O
Lord."

MARCH 26th

DAVID THE AGED   *Reading: 1 Kings 1. 1–4.*

We have now come to David's last days on earth. The story
is not a very pleasant one, for we see him so feeble that only
Abishag can warm him, and so slow of decision that if Nathan
had not acted boldly the wrong son would have made himself
king. One wonders if it would not have been kinder to have
drawn a veil over the declining days of a man who had
previously been so magnificent, but perhaps the purpose of
this disclosure is to stress that even in physical and mental
deterioration David remained spiritually strong. The man
whom the world might have dubbed senile was able to rise
up in his bed to charge his successor, Solomon, to be strong
and to show himself a man in obeying God's commands. This
gives us a wonderful illustration of the fact that old age does
not affect the believer's true spiritual life.

MARCH 27th

DEBORAH   *Reading: Judges 5. 1–7.*

Some have felt that it was very much to Israel's discredit that they had to be ruled by a woman, feeling sure that this represented something less than the divine order. However, the main purpose of the book of Judges is to magnify God's grace in using unsuitable people for His work. Some of them put their more orthodox critics to shame. Was it any discredit to Deborah that rather than allow God's people to be treated as slaves she accepted a "mother's" responsibility? She may not have been an ideal judge but at least she did not passively accept defeat as the men did. There is another point to be noted: the fact that Barak ultimately emerged as a hero of faith (Hebrews 11. 32) was almost entirely due to Deborah's influence. To inspire faith in others, as well as to have it oneself, is surely a great achievement.

MARCH 28th

DELILAH   *Reading: Judges 16. 4–21.*

We could be shocked at the mention of "love" in this sordid story if our modern civilisation did not misuse this noble word in the same way. We might also be shocked at Delilah's callous behaviour in her lust for money if we did not live in an age when gambling is a major industry. Just as Delilah cared nothing for what Samson lost so long as she scooped the Philistine jackpot, so today people plunge into every kind of effort to get rich quickly, without pausing to consider that they can only do so by impoverishing others. When each of the Philistine lords had handed over his bribe Delilah must have been quite a rich woman. Perhaps in consequence she acquired sufficient status to be among the three thousand spectators who mocked at Samson. If so she soon learned that the wages of sin may sometimes be shekels but is always death.

MARCH 29th

DEMAS   *Reading: 2 Timothy 4. 9–18.*

Demas may have left Rome because he was a disheartened man. The gospel was perhaps not producing much effect there, and it is possible that he found it difficult to live in close association with Paul at that period. All the other workers had scattered except Luke, and he must have felt lonely. He may have missed the bright singing, the constant excitement of new converts and the thrilling Second Advent meetings in Thessalonica, for that was where he went when he left Rome. How many since Demas have found that their own locality or assembly was dull and uninspiring, and instead of doggedly going on have moved away to join a more prosperous or exciting church elsewhere? If this is what happened, Demas no doubt excused himself, as we would, with some pious phrases, but Paul classed his departure as rank unfaithfulness.

MARCH 30th

DEMETRIUS   *Reading: Acts 19. 24–41.*

Demetrius is typical of the man who has no logical argument and so resorts to abuse. Such men engender an emotional atmosphere which inflames whole groups of people and gets them shouting empty slogans which have no real meaning. We see the devastation wrought by such agitators today as they stir up trouble and violence just as Demetrius did in Ephesus. The last thing that such a man will do is to reason calmly, or to reason at all: he must have denunciations and heated shouting down of his opponents. Such actions are not altogether unknown in our own churches. It is true that the Ephesian uproar was made by pagans over a false religion, but among Christians there have been quarrels connected with the true faith which have been just as senseless and almost as cruel.

MARCH 31st

DIDYMUS *Reading: John 11. 1–16.*

Since there is no reference to the other twin we wonder why Thomas was spoken of and remembered by this surname of Didymus, the Twin. Within himself Thomas could perhaps be said to have had twin features. One twin was devotion; he was ready to die for his Lord. The other was doubt, for he had a propensity for taking the gloomy view and fearing the worst. Unhappily doubt suppressed devotion. Take the occasion at Bethany, when Thomas's obvious willingness to sacrifice all for Christ was overshadowed by his dreary anticipation that their mission was about to meet a violent end. Doubt must have received a setback by what happened, but in a few days its grimmest forebodings seemed all too justified. It was only by the resurrection that doubt was quenched and devotion released. Devotion and doubt are uneasy twins. The proper companion for devotion is faith.

APRIL 1st

DIONYSIUS *Reading: Acts 17. 18–34.*

Had it been possible for the world by its own wisdom to know God, then Athens would have been the city and the Areopagus the place where that knowledge would have been obtained. The outcome of Paul's preaching there, however, proved that this crowd of philosophers and poets who sat around on the historic stone tiers of Mars Hill were farther from God than the corrupt cosmopolitans of Corinth. To be invited to preach in that august assembly promised to be the greatest moment in Paul's life, but in the event it turned out to be one of his greatest disappointments. In the seat of classical learning he proved what foolishness the gospel is to human wisdom. Dionysius was the exception which redeemed the occasion. This one convert made it all worthwhile.

APRIL 2nd

DIOTREPHES   *Reading: 3 John 1–11.*

John was right to be indignant about the behaviour of Diotrephes, since the only scriptural reasons for excluding a believer from an assembly are false doctrine or scandalous behaviour. It is difficult to know just how Diotrephes came to acquire the personal authority which made his action possible. Obviously changes were beginning to take place in the churches if one man could behave himself in this high-handed way. Under some pretext or other he had become the sole authority in his church. He enjoyed power; which of us does not? He abused his power; which of us would not do that if it were not for the restraint of our fellow Christians? The practice of fellowship would have saved Diotrephes from his abiding stigma. Fellowship is the God-given safe-guard for us all.

APRIL 3rd

DOEG   *Reading: Psalm 52. 1–5.*

According to the title given to this psalm David wrote it on receipt of the news of the disastrous tale-bearing of Doeg the Edomite (1 Samuel 22. 20–23). There are few things more murderous in their effect than malicious gossip. Doeg's tongue was as cruel as his sword, and as disastrous as a slashing razor. Since the information which he gave was correct it may seem unfair to describe his words as "lying", but there can be no question as to the evil intention which prompted his betrayal. Sometimes the worst type of scandal-mongering is the unkind exposure of other people's private affairs. We are not surprised, and nor was David, that Doeg the tale-bearer later became Doeg the assassin. So often there is a murderous nature behind that malicious tongue.

APRIL 4th

DORCAS   *Reading: Acts 9. 26–43.*

Peter did not need a new coat. If he had, Dorcas would doubtless have found much pleasure in making one for him. What he did need, though, was a new experience of God's miracle-working power to fortify him for the crisis which lay ahead at Caesarea. There was one way by which Dorcas could make this possible, and that was by her death. Strangely enough, her dying brought more Joppa people to a living faith in Christ than all her good works had done. Of course the value was not in her death, but in the subsequent experience of Christ's resurrection power. God had been willing to suspend her good works in order to do in her and through her what could have been done in no other way. It was also an inspiring experience for Peter, preparing him for the call to Caesarea with its tremendous implications.

APRIL 5th

EBED-MELECH   *Reading: Jeremiah 38. 1–13.*

In addition to having a commendation from God, Jeremiah had a big "Thank you" himself for Ebed-melech, who had rescued him from a living death. He had cause to appreciate especially the cast-off and rotten rags which had been used in his rescue. It was good of the resourceful slave to think of them. It is, of course, possible that the thirty men with their cords could have extricated the prophet from his miry dungeon without them, but it would have been a painful experience for him. That idea of putting the rags under his armpits showed that the Ethiopian eunuch was not only courageous but sensitive. It was an extra bit of care and it serves to remind us that people not only need dragging up out of the mud; they need to be treated gently in the process. It didn't cost more than a little thoughtfulness.

APRIL 6th

EHUD   *Reading: Judges 3. 15–26.*

The book of Judges deals with lawless times, so we must not be surprised to read of political assassination. Nor must we be surprised to read of a deliverer who suffered from a physical handicap, since all the judges had some kind of disadvantage. Ehud's particular handicap was that he could not use his right hand in any effective way. He was able to turn this to positive advantage. It never occurred to king Eglon's security guard to suspect a concealed weapon on his right hip, for no normal man could snatch a dagger from there. So they wrongly judged him to be unarmed when they allowed him to have a private interview with the tyrant, with the result which we know. What we may not know is that in more peaceful ways our personal handicaps may often be made to serve God's purposes.

APRIL 7th

ELDAD   *Reading: Numbers 11. 24–30.*

Eldad was a victim of the all too common demand that spiritual experiences should be uniform. People seem to think that spiritual power must always express itself in the same way. For some reason Eldad was not present when the sixty eight others received their "anointing". Neither the young man who ran to tell Moses nor the scandalised Joshua questioned the fact of Eldad's calling or the reality of his prophesying; what they objected to was his unorthodoxy. Moses rightly silenced these critics. The Spirit must be allowed to bless and use men in His own way, without deferring to our petty demands for stereotyped procedure. Why must Eldad copy other people's experience or conform to their pattern? He is a man of the Spirit. Let us rejoice and leave it at that.

APRIL 8th

ELIAB   *Reading: 1 Samuel 16. 1–7.*

Samuel was all unconsciously looking for a man as tall and handsome as Saul, so he immediately presumed that Jesse's eldest son, Eliab, was the man to be anointed. God, however, has other ways of judging and He knew that Eliab was a man of a jealous disposition, and not therefore to be considered as king. It is striking that the wise and godly old prophet, Samuel, could make such a mistake as to feel sure that Eliab was his man. It reminds us that even the most spiritually experienced can judge wrongly. The essential mark of true spirituality is not infallible judgment, but a readiness to be corrected. Samuel had this, and so was saved from a wrong decision. However imposing Eliab was, he was not the man for this position; and in such matters, God cares nothing for seniority.

APRIL 9th

ELIEZAR   *Reading: Genesis 24. 34–48.*

Eliezar of Damascus was Abraham's trusted steward (Genesis 15. 2). In this story he gives a graphic picture of the ideal servant. He can be trusted with all his master's wealth, he is shrewd in his dealings with men, and he is so conscientious that he will not eat before stating his business nor delay when the matter is settled. Above all he makes every action a matter of prayer and does not forget to pause and give thanks when prayer is answered. When the task is completed he reports to his master and then fades into the background. Most remarkable of all, no mention is made of his name throughout the whole story. Many have regarded him as a type of the Holy Spirit seeking a bride for the Father's Son. He is certainly an example for anyone who aspires to be a Spirit-filled steward of God's grace.

APRIL 10th

ELIHU   *Reading: Job 37. 1–7.*

In the middle of the nineteenth century a British official in
Bengal, India, established a system of finger-print identifi-
cation. It is said that he had his attention drawn to this matter
by Elihu's words. This young man followed up the lengthy
arguments of Job's three friends with his own forceful contribution concerning the inscrutable greatness of God. Among
many other proofs he stated that the Almighty has put His
seal of individuality on every man's hand. Whether Elihu's
words gave the clue to modern science or not they allude to
the amazing phenomenon that no two men have identical
fingerprints. True faith always emphasises that it is a sacred
and significant fact that God never deals with humanity "en
masse", but gives individual dignity to all.

APRIL 11th

ELIJAH (i)   *Reading: 1 Kings 17. 17–24.*

The great point at issue in Elijah's ministry was the proof that
God is a living God. Elijah boldly stated this as a fact but it
had to be proved, firstly in private and then before the world.
Now there is only one sure way of proving the resurrection
power of God and that is by being led into difficulties for
which there is no human solution. That is why Elijah was
sent to Cherith and afterwards to Sidon, there to be confronted with the daily challenge of the empty meal barrel and
later with the major crisis of the dead boy. Having thus
proved God in private he was ready for the test on Carmel,
where he was able to display a relaxed confidence in God's
absolute power. He was able to show the whole nation that
the Almighty God is alive, because he already had a secret
history with God in his personal affairs.

APRIL 12th

ELIJAH (ii)   *Reading: 1 Kings 19. 1–8.*

Elijah once stumbled wearily on to a piece of waste ground, threw himself under a tree in despair at his own overwhelming failure and wished that he were dead. The same Elijah was subsequently privileged to stand on a mountain peak with the bright glow of heaven all around and the King of kings standing at his side. What was it that lifted this man from the depths of suicidal despair to the height of superlative success? It was the grace of God. This grace soothed him, fed him, whispered to him in love, renewed his hope, strengthened him to go on, and finally snatched him up to heaven. If any still ask the question, "Where is the Lord God of Elijah?" the answer is that He is very near to each of us and is ready to do these very same things so that one day we, too, may stand with Christ in glory.

APRIL 13th

ELISABETH   *Reading: Luke 1. 35–45.*

Mary had suffered a great shock with the astounding news of her Spirit-given pregnancy. Happily there was a home up in the Judean hills where she knew that she could find help, so she hurried there, and must have been delighted as well as surprised to find that Elisabeth knew all about it. We are not told how she knew, only that she was able to give Mary just the comfort and encouragement which she needed before having to face Joseph with the news. Elisabeth must have lived very close to God for her home of all the homes in Israel to be the one chosen by heaven as a haven for this perplexed young woman. There was no need for Elisabeth to envy her husband's official position in the temple; she had a ministry of exceptional importance in her own home, where Mary found sanctuary.

APRIL 14th

ELISHA (i)   *Reading: 2 Kings 4. 42–44.*

Elisha had Elijah's mantle and a double portion of his spirit, yet he was an entirely different kind of man. Elijah was a striking character, a wanderer, a man rough in his manner of life and unpredictable in his movements. Elisha had a quiet, unimposing appearance, regular habits and calm temperament. He was no wanderer, but could often be found resting on a bed or sitting in his house. It was not that Elisha had less power than Elijah; far from it. It was simply that the Spirit of God expressed Himself in different manners in the two men. This is very important. It was not for Elisha to attempt to copy Elijah, for this would have been artificial. God does not have stereotyped servants; He has men and women with their own personalities. Elisha's secret of Spirit-filled service was just to be himself.

APRIL 15th

ELISHA (ii)   *Reading: 2 Kings 13. 14–21.*

Elisha never lost his experience of the fulness of the Spirit. Now spiritual energy is quite different from mere natural vigour. When Elisha was lying sick on his death bed he had more energy than the virile king Joash. He could only rest his feeble hands on the martial hands of the king for the token shooting of the arrow, but he could flare up into hot indignation at the thought of only a partial victory. When he died and his bones lay in a grave there was still a life-giving potency in them, as was accidentally proved by the burial party of another man. All of which goes to prove that the spiritual power which had been so evident in his lifetime was the result of God's working through him. Spiritual power did not proceed from Elisha, but it originated with God who was pleased to use the prophet as a means of communication.

APRIL 16th

ELKANAH   *Reading: 1 Samuel 1. 21–28.*

Elkanah was clearly a man of a kindly disposition towards
other people and a sincere devotion to his God. Somehow,
though, he did not seem to have the spiritual vigour required
for their family crisis, so Hannah had to provide what he
lacked. The most that Elkanah could do was to show affection
and understanding as she battled her way through alone,
though after the birth of Samuel he was as concerned as she
was that her vow to the Lord should be faithfully fulfilled.
Her faith must have made a great impression on him. The
story begins with the fact that he loved her dearly and finishes
by showing how much he also came to respect her. Happy
indeed is any marriage where trials and difficulties are sur-
mounted not only with undiminished affection but also with
increasing mutual respect.

APRIL 17th

ENOCH   *Reading: Genesis 5. 18–24.*

Enoch so kept step with God on earth that one day the two
of them walked right on into heaven together. Why was it so
unusual at that time to find a man who walked with God?
Firstly because to walk with another means to desire the same
destination. God's end is fixed, and He will not vary it.
Secondly because it also involves taking the same route—not
only to desire God's end but to be willing for God's way.
Thirdly because it means to go at the same pace—too fast
leaves your companion behind, while too slow leaves you
behind. If you cannot vary your pace to God's, you will soon
part company. Enoch accepted these conditions and he
enjoyed his journeyings right through to the end. God seems
equally to have found pleasure in the company of His walking
companion. Since Enoch many others have pursued life's
journey in the same way.

EPHRAIM   *Reading: 1 Chronicles 7. 20–22.*

Jacob's prophecies concerning his grandson Ephraim spoke not only of his taking precedence over his elder brother, but also of his future supremacy among the ten tribes. Ephraim was to be very great (Genesis 48. 19). All this was ultimately fulfilled, although the next phase of his life brought the great set-back occasioned by the sudden death of two of his sons. It is noteworthy that they were killed in a foray by which they hoped to increase the family wealth. Poor Ephraim evidently felt this bereavement keenly, and was no doubt surprised and disappointed to find his family diminishing instead of increasing. He had to learn—as we all do—that to grasp for more often means loss rather than gain, even though promises of enlargement seem to justify the action. God's promises are fulfilled by His faithfulness and not by our strivings.

APRIL 19th

EPAPHRODITUS   *Reading: Philippians 4. 13–18.*

Wherever Epaphroditus went, he carried with him an atmosphere of sweet fragrance which reached right up to heaven. As he travelled from Philippi to Rome he carried the church's sacrificial gifts to provide for Paul's needs. As he travelled back from Rome he himself constituted a sacrificial gift to the believers in Philippi, for Paul confessed that he would much rather have retained this valued fellow-soldier for his own company. Epaphroditus, however, not only carried fragrance, but also emitted it by being ready to give his own life in glad service to others for Christ's sake. To God there is no fragrance so sweet as that of practical love among His children. He is not impressed by fair words and pious wishes, but He treasures that love in action which releases the authentic perfume of His Son.

APRIL 20th

ESAU *Reading: Genesis 33. 1–11.*

A strong and energetic sportsman, Esau had neither time nor inclination for spiritual things. Like many other materialists, he prospered greatly and became a man of considerable possessions. Although he lost the spiritual value of his despised birthright, he actually inherited not just the double portion but the whole of his father's wealth, for Jacob got nothing from Isaac, their father. So affluent was Esau that he waved aside the handsome present which Jacob brought him, though he was ready enough to be pressed to take it. Is it possible that, when God sees that a man cannot be induced to take any interest in eternal things, then He lets him have temporal ease and prosperity? Let us note, however, that such prosperity is no mark of the divine favour.

APRIL 21st

ESTHER *Reading: Esther 5. 1–8.*

Esther was not only attractive and patriotic, she was disciplined. She refrained from asking for more than the presence of the king and Haman at her banquet, in spite of the generous invitation to ask what she would. Her invitation was accepted, and as they sat at the feast Esther could see that the king was in a mood to give her almost anything. Instead of voicing her petition, though, she contented herself with what must have seemed a feeble or foolish request for a further banquet. From then on things happened speedily; the erection of the gallows by Haman, the king's sleepless night, his decision to honour Mordecai. For the third time Esther was urged to state her request, and as she did so God began His mighty deliverance. It takes a really disciplined spirit to wait for God's time.

APRIL 22nd

EUNICE *Reading: Acts 16. 1–3.*

We know from Paul's letter that Timothy's mother's name was Eunice, which means "a good victory" or, as we might say, "an overcomer". She was a Jewess married to a man of a different religion. This might not have mattered much if she had not become a Christian, but unhappily the gospel can produce a divided home. When Eunice heard the gospel she was already married, so any division in her home was not of her making. It could not have been easy to be true to Christ, but she found grace to do so, and even if she did not win her husband to Christ she had the joy of seeing their son become a true servant of the Lord. The hardest battlefield for any woman in Eunice's position must be her own home. There she is called to be a true overcomer—both a good wife and a good Christian.

APRIL 23rd

EVE *Reading: Genesis 2. 18–25.*

Why did Satan speak only to Eve? Possibly because he saw how Adam loved her and listened to her gentle counsel. As the devil cunningly considered the couple, he decided that Eve was the partner with influence, and that Adam could be persuaded if only Eve could be deceived (1 Timothy 2. 14). He was right, but the pity was that Eve used her influence for harm and not for good. That the wife should have had so much influence over her husband was no criticism, but a compliment. It ought, however, to have humbled her and driven her to her knees in earnest prayer that she might indeed be a "help meet" for him. To be loved by a good man brings responsibilities as well as pleasure, responsibilities so great that only deep dependence on God can be sufficient.

APRIL 24th

EZEKIEL (i)   *Reading: Ezekiel 1. 15–28.*

Ezekiel began his work for God with an extraordinary vision
of wheels: enormous wheels, wheels with eyes, whirling
wheels, and wheels within wheels; they were the wheels of
God. Their message was that God's purposes roll on to
realisation and nothing can stop them. Jerusalem fell, but still
they spun round. Although Ezekiel himself was dumb for a
time the wheels still kept moving. The prophet was a methodical man, as is revealed by his habit of constantly noting the
date of the various events. Whenever he recorded another
day, he reminded himself with confidence that whatever
else was happening God's wheels were still revolving. God,
too, is methodical. He always has a purpose for each day.
His wheels roll on, directed as always by the heavenly Man
on the throne, even our Lord Jesus.

APRIL 25th

EZEKIEL (ii)   *Reading: Ezekiel 24. 15–24.*

How often a man's domestic affairs give value to his spiritual
ministry! Isaiah with his children, Jeremiah with his celibacy,
Hosea with his broken home: each of them found that there
is no division between the secular and the sacred, between a
man's private life and his work for God. Ezekiel had to bear
the sudden death of his adored wife and use the occasion to
illustrate his message to the people. Is this, then, what it means
to be a "sign", bringing into view not one's self importance
but one's sorrows? Does it have to be by suffering that point
and validity are given to a man's preaching? It does seem that
this is often God's method. The man who is to speak words
of lasting helpfulness to others is the man who has himself
been through the deeps with God.

APRIL 26th

EZRA   *Reading: Ezra 8. 15–31.*

We can understand Ezra being ashamed at the sinfulness of his people (9.6) but it is unusual to find a man who is "ashamed" to ask the world for help. His conviction and his experience were that God's hand was upon him for good; how then could he turn away from that loving hand to get assistance from the hand of a merely earthly king? That was the right kind of shame, to be ashamed of grieving the Lord. Ezra was also ashamed that it should ever be thought that he doubted God. He had given a bold testimony in words as to God's sufficiency, so it was important not to contradict that testimony by his actions. He was ashamed to give men the chance to think that in a time of crisis he abandoned his faith in the omnipotent hand of God. This would be a shameful thing for any of us.

APRIL 27th

FELIX   *Reading: Acts 24. 10–27.*

The Latin word means "happy", but if ever a man was misnamed it was Felix. He began his life as a slave, but was made a freedman by the emperor Claudius. Tacitus, the Roman historian, remarked of him that although he rose to be a king there was a slave's heart hidden all the time under his royal robes. He was a slave to the Jewish people, for while he governed them he tried to ingratiate himself with them. He was a slave to his troubled conscience and trembled at Paul's words. He was a slave to Drusilla, a woman of abandoned life who was another man's wife. Right to the end of his stay in Caesarea he was a slave to sordid money. Paul witnessed to him, reasoned with him and certainly prayed for him, but it was all in vain. A man can only be truly happy if he is committed to Christ.

APRIL 28th

FORTUNATUS   *Reading: 1 Corinthians 16. 15–24.*

Not all devoted Christians are refreshing people to meet.
Fortunatus and his two companions are recorded as being men
who acted like a tonic to the spirit of Paul. These men made
the hearts of their Christian friends feel lighter by their very
presence. What was the secret of Fortunatus' cheering influence? It was not natural lightheartedness, for it was Paul's
spirit which was refreshed as well as his soul. It was not that he
brought a glowing report of God's work, for things were not
good at Corinth just then. It was certainly not some deep
teaching from the Bible, for Paul already had much more of
that than Fortunatus would ever know. It must have been his
pre-occupation with the Lord Jesus. There is nothing like the
love of Christ to act as a tonic to a jaded spirit.

APRIL 29th

GAD THE SEER   *Reading: 2 Samuel 24. 11–19.*

Unhappy Gad saw his royal master fall into a serious fault,
and he had to face David with three grim alternatives. It must
have been a heartbreaking experience after their close comradeship of many years, and it speaks well for both of the men
that they got through it together. With what earnest prayer
the seer must have cried to God about it all, and with what joy
returned to take back a message of hope to the stricken king!
He encouraged David to build an altar in Ornan's threshing
floor and used his foresight in the securing of the site for the
future temple. We are later told that he helped David to
arrange the temple music (2 Chronicles 29. 25). It is sometimes
a painful business to be a seer, but it is a rewarding one when
the vision leads away from man's failure to God's mercy and
God's glory.

APRIL 30th

GAIUS THE HOST *Reading: Romans 16. 23.*

Gaius was noted for his hospitality. It was a great compliment to be singled out as "my host" by the apostle Paul, but the Holy Spirit is careful to point out that Gaius kept open house for the whole church. It may indicate that the church held its meetings in his house. In any case we may be sure that wherever Paul stayed it had to be an open house to all believers and enquirers so that he would always be available. Perhaps when Gaius first invited Paul to share his home he did not realise what a continual coming and going of others would be involved. Such hospitality is not easy. It means hard work, long hours, constant expense and many petty inconveniences. The more credit, then, to Gaius and his wife who carried on in this way, and credit also to those in the twentieth century who follow their example.

MAY 1st

GAIUS THE BELOVED *Reading: 3 John 1–8.*

There are those who regard bodily weakness as a proof of low spirituality, attributing every sickness to a lamentable lack of faith. The apostle John was not among this number. He was particularly impressed with the healthy spiritual condition of his good friend Gaius, though sorry about his natural weakness. As he gave thanks to God for this faithful Christian brother he also prayed for him, and was led to make his chief request that Gaius' physical condition might improve. It was a suitable prayer, for the Holy Spirit can overflow from our hearts into our very bodies with His living power. But let not the healed or healthy imagine that they are superior to their less physically robust brothers and sisters, or more spiritual than they. The very opposite may be true. A healthy body can contain a sick soul.

MAY 2nd

GALLIO *Reading: Acts 18. 12–17.*

If Gallio had been a Festus, then Paul, with his work for God still incomplete, might have found himself obliged to appeal to Caesar in Rome. It is in accordance with the amazing over-ruling of God's providence that even Roman governors, with their diverse temperaments, contributed to the outworking of divine plans. Supposing that Pilate had been a man like Gallio! He would never have been intimidated by the Jews, Christ would not have been handed over to death, and there would have been no Cross. It would be idle to make these speculations but for the fact that they emphasise how the natural characteristics of a new pro-consul served the purposes of God. Gallio was well known as a kind but firm ruler, and this action which kept Paul free to preach the gospel was in keeping with his character.

MAY 3rd

GAMALIEL *Reading: Acts 5. 36–40.*

The Jews had a special title, Rabban, which they reserved for their seven most worthy teachers. Gamaliel's learning was so eminent and his character so revered that he was one of the seven. The best virtues which Saul of Tarsus learned from Judaism were taught him by this great master, and it seems possible that it was from him, too, that Saul first acquired his strong confidence in the absolute sovereignty of God. We wonder why Gamaliel did not himself become a Christian. Perhaps it was because he could never bring himself to bow to the risen Christ as "Rabboni". In any case it is a strange fact that there is more hope of the conversion of a fanatical opponent of the gospel like Saul, than of a man like Gamaliel who could tolerate it but never commit himself to it.

MAY 4th

GEDALIAH   *Reading: Jeremiah 40. 7–16.*

We know little about Gedaliah who ruled the remnant of Jews for seven short months, except that he was an upright man, doing his best to encourage order and honest work, but soon swept away by the backlash of violence and intrigue which followed the withdrawal of the Babylonian armies. He was, perhaps, foolish to disbelieve the security reports given to him, but in any case he would not permit plotting and murder by those under his command. The threat was all too real and his regime came to a violent end. Nevertheless he was surely right to refuse to keep himself in office by scheming and violence. The message which he leaves to us is that if we become involved in situations of defeat and disruption we should face them with the dignity and integrity which befits servants of God.

MAY 5th

GEHAZI   *Reading: 2 Kings 4. 25–37.*

When Elisha stood on the bank of the Jordan and touched the water with Elijah's robe, the waters were divided. When Gehazi entered the house at Shunem and laid Elisha's staff on the face of the dead child, nothing happened. The reason for this contrast is that Elisha had then become a man of God, filled with the same Spirit as his master, whereas Gehazi was only a man of God's servant; he never made the grade of being a man of God himself. If only he had sought a double portion of his master's spirit, as Elisha had, he might have received power; but instead he remained powerless, because when the choice came he showed himself to be governed by self interest. When Naaman's gifts were refused by Elisha, Gehazi schemed and lied to get some of them for himself and even used God's name in justification (2 Kings 5. 20). Such a man cannot be trusted with spiritual power.

MAY 6th

GERSHOM   *Reading: Exodus 2. 15–22.*

When Moses threw in his lot with the people of God he became a man without a home. As he left Egypt he must have been oppressed by his compatriots' ingratitude, and might be forgiven if he had resolved never to help anybody else again. However it was instinctive in him to champion the weak, so that when he arrived in Midian and found Reuel's daughters in trouble he gave them help and was taken into their home. He gained a wife and a son, but, in giving the name Gershom to the boy, he betrayed his wistfulness at being unsettled. This name set a pattern for the rest of his life, for from that time onwards Moses never had a fixed home. Yet no man, except the homeless Son of Man, ever lived so near to God. Gershom reminds us that the man who has his home in God is always a stranger and a pilgrim in his contemporary world.

MAY 7th

GIDEON (i)   *Reading: Judges 6. 27–34.*

In his day Gideon was the embodiment of that slightly ridiculous figure, the little man. He was as painfully aware of his inadequacy as was everybody else. Then God met him, and he did the outrageous act which none of the larger characters around him had ever dared to do—he defied the indecent Baal. His father was greatly impressed; he soon silenced the complaining neighbours and gave his young son the nickname of Jerubbaal. The name stuck. It was the name of the man who had pricked the bubble of popular superstition and exposed its futility. Gideon was to have many greater victories than this, but always in the same role of the little man. God wanted him like that. God kept him like that, even to the extent of reducing his army to less than one per cent of its strength. He prefers "the things that are not" as instruments for His triumphs.

MAY 8th

GIDEON (ii)   *Reading: Judges 6. 33–40.*

The contrasting experiences of Gideon's fleece gave a double
confirmation to his faith, and they can also illustrate what
may happen to any preacher. Such a man may feel sure that
the anointing power of the Spirit is on him as, in spite of the
lack of any outward helps, he finds freshness and fluency in
speaking God's word. Such a man finds the abundance of
heavenly dew to be very inspiring. Then a doubt may arise
in his mind, as he wonders whether after all his apparent
anointing is just an expression of natural facility. In this case
the second sign will help him, if he finds that in spite of all his
advantages and efforts there is little "dew" and he knows himself to be dry, like the fleece. This is a painful sign, but ought
to be a comfort to the man who desires only the authentic
power of the Spirit in his ministry.

MAY 9th

GIDEON (iii)   *Reading: Judges 7. 16–22.*

The newly posted sentries of the Midianites must have calculated that any army which could supply three hundred
trumpeters and operate boldly with bright lights must be of
vast proportions. They little knew that Gideon and his men
had nothing behind them but God. Now that we know the
outcome we can relish the idea of this circle of men with a
light in one hand and a trumpet in the other being regarded as an
army at all. It was a gigantic bit of bluff and it came off, but
only because of the iron discipline of this group of nobodies.
If Gideon had flinched or retreated, the whole enterprise would
have finished in a fiasco. He stood his ground, and so did they
all, and God did the rest. We feeble Christians can also have
God behind us if we keep our eyes on our heavenly Captain
and stand firmly together for Him. If God is not behind us we
have nothing else.

MAY 10th

GOLIATH   *Reading: 1 Samuel 17. 41–51.*

Goliath was more than life size. He was large and loud, arrogant and boastful. He had a lust for publicity, making sure that everyone knew his height and the weight of his weapons. He spoke contemptuously of his opponents and roared out his oaths at the slightest sign of opposition. Yet he was strangely uneasy when he was confronted by a man who refused to employ his methods and his weapons, relying simply on humility and faith in God. This was a way of life completely alien to Goliath, and it worried him. More, it defeated him in a way which made him look clumsy and ridiculous. This is more than an exciting story; it is a challenge to us all. Later David confessed that God's gentleness has made him great (2 Samuel 22. 36). His was true greatness and was the very opposite of the giant's inflated self-assertion.

MAY 11th

GOMER   *Reading: Hosea 2. 1–7.*

It is a difficult life for any woman to be married to a prophet. However considerate he may be, the fact remains that he is so pre-occupied with his work for God that he cannot give his wife the little extra attentions which mean so much to a woman. Most prophets are poor men; they forego the increasing prosperity which normally makes life easier as the years go by. Gomer never had a heart for the things of God, so may well have resented her lot. It was then that other men came along with their flattering attentions and their inflated purses. She yielded to them, first with surreptitious unfaithfulness and then with a life of open shame. It seems clear that her first act of deceit took place while she was still at home with her husband, but she finished in the slave market. The first resentment, the first indulgence, the first lie will lead to utter shame if they are not resisted.

MAY 12th

HABAKKUK   *Reading: Habakkuk 2. 1–4.*

As Habakkuk was on his watch tower he was told that the just man must learn to live by faith alone. He tried it, and found that as the days grew even darker his heart was at rest and he was able to rejoice when everybody else was in despair. He passed on the message, and centuries later Paul received it. He tried it and found that faith in the living God gave him fulness of life. He also passed on the message and again, centuries later, Martin Luther received it. His soul darkness had been as black as Habakkuk's and Paul's, but faith brought him through also and gave him a song of praise. Luther passed it on. Wesley received it and he began to sing too. It has come down to us, and we need it as much as any of them ever did. Dark days may be coming on us, and only a living faith can enable us to sing our way through to victory. We too must pass it on.

MAY 13th

HAGAR   *Reading: Genesis 16. 6–13.*

Writers who wish to denigrate Victorian piety often make sneering allusions to wall texts with pictures of a terrifying eye and an inscription, "Thou God Seest Me". No doubt there have been people guilty of interpreting these words as a threat, but their speaker, Hagar, had no such emotion. On the contrary she found deep comfort in the realisation that, although she was far from human compassion or help, she had God's loving attention and His kind care. Considering the harsh treatment she had received from her mistress, Sarai, she might have wondered if God did see or care. Here was she, a pregnant refugee, alone in her distress. There was, however, an eye which looked kindly on her and an ear which listened to her sighs. What is more, there was a heart of love planning for her future. That is what she meant by the grateful confession, "Thou God seest me."

MAY 14th

HAGGAI *Reading: Haggai 1. 1–14.*

To Haggai there was only one explanation of the economic misfortunes of the Jews; it was their lack of devotion to God's house. Equally there was one radical solution to all of their problems; it was that they should devote themselves to its rebuilding. He had no time for the arguments of those who pointed out the political complications. He was not at all affected by their pleas of being too busy or too poor. To him it was a straightforward matter of priorities. Get your priorities right, he kept repeating, and all else will be well. He so lived what he preached that his earnestness became contagious. A few forceful words from him brought rulers and people together in a concerted effort, and, as soon as they started building, God's presence and power were known among them. Our priority is not a building but the living fellowship of believers.

MAY 15th

HAM *Reading: Genesis 9. 18–27.*

Strange as it may seem, there are some Bible readers who maintain that the African peoples ought to remain permanently second-class human beings because of Noah's curse on his son Canaan. It is difficult to base anything on the first words of a man just waking up from a drunken stupor, and it seems much more logical and just to blame Noah for the squalid scene in his bedroom. Nevertheless there may have been something prophetical in his outburst, for perhaps there are descendants of Ham still, men who are black not in skin but in heart. These are the real descendants of Ham, these men of any colour whose imagination is defiled by lewdness, and who contaminate the atmosphere around them with coarse talk and obscene gloating. In this sense there was a deal of truth in Noah's words, for the curse of right judgment rests upon them, and their filthiness makes them the basest of slaves.

MAY 16th

HAMAN *Reading: Esther 3. 1–11.*

But for the merciful intervention of God, Haman would have destroyed Mordecai the Benjamite; indeed, because of Mordecai, this descendant of Agag planned to liquidate the whole Jewish nation. Much earlier God had commanded Saul to destroy the Amalekites and their king Agag. Saul, who was himself a Benjamite, disobeyed this command and was severely censured for his action (1 Samuel 15. 9). To us it may seem to have been harsh, but we are now confronted with the fact that Haman the Agagite almost brought about the destruction of this leading Benjamite and all the rest too. This happening, after so many years, is a startling reminder of how the disobedience of long ago can catch up with us and bring ruin. Men sow trouble for themselves which they will later reap if they disobey God. Happily the book of Esther encourages us to believe in God's mercy and His power to deliver.

MAY 17th

HANAMEL *Reading: Jeremiah 32. 6–15.*

It may well be that this rather slick young man was among the majority who scoffed at Jeremiah's prophecy of total defeat. In any case he judged it safer to take no chances, and felt that ready cash was preferable to title deeds at such a time of uncertainty. By Jewish law he could not sell outside his family, so he decided that Uncle Jeremiah might be soft enough to do a deal. Jeremiah bought the land from Hanamel, not because he was a speculator but because he was a serious investor. He knew that he would never possess the family farm, but he invested his seventeen shekels in the Bank of Faith. The investment is still paying rich dividends by the comfort which the story gives to multitudes of tried believers, and the capital is still safe in heaven, together with that of all others who have been convinced that there is nothing too hard for God.

MAY 18th

HANNAH   *Reading: 1 Samuel 2. 1–11.*

A song suddenly rang out sweet and clear above the hubbub of worshippers; it was a song which has thrilled believers ever since, and which obviously provided the basis for Mary's Magnificat. Hannah, who had sighed and wept on her previous visit to the house of God, now sang for joy. She did not mind now that her rival wife had provoked her, for it had driven her to pray through to God, unhelped even by the high priest. Her prayer had been heard and little Samuel was the answer. For some years she had cared for him at home and had loved every minute of it, but now he was big enough for her to fulfil her vow of giving him back to God. She sang, although she was going back to an empty home. This was the purest joy of all, the joy not of receiving but of giving. Her home was not empty for long since God gave her more children, so showing how greatly He loves a cheerful giver.

MAY 19th

HEROD THE GREAT   *Reading: Matthew 2. 7–18.*

We know enough of Herod the Great to realise that this murderous action was typical: he had his second wife, Mariamne I, falsely accused and executed; towards the end of his reign he grew insanely jealous of her two sons and murdered them; then, in a frenzied fear of plots, he turned on the son of his first wife and had him killed. Soon after this the Magi arrived with their story, so the cunning and murderous Herod did exactly what might have been expected of him by slaughtering the Bethlehem children. Later he was taken with a loathsome mortal disease: even as he was dying he gave orders for a number of Jewish leaders in Jericho to be executed when death came, to make sure that there would be mourning in Judea, even though not for him. Actually this was not carried out, but it all serves as incidental proof of the Bible's accuracy.

MAY 20th

HEROD ANTIPAS   *Reading: Luke 23. 6-12.*

This Herod was the son of Herod the Great by yet another
wife, a Samaritan. He had the distinction of being coldly
ignored by the compassionate Christ who never turned away
even from the worst of sinners. Jesus called Herod Antipas a
sly "fox" and did not judge him to be worth a single word.
Herod tried to cover his mortification by mocking, yet he who
had been frightened by John's hot denunciation may well have
been terrified by this icy contempt. However unlikely a listener
might be, and even though words of reproof had to be said,
Jesus always spoke, so long as there was any chance of saving
a man from himself. To Herod He had nothing to say; this
man was so insincere that he was best treated with silence. The
Romans seemed to have the same opinion of him, for they
banished him to Gaul, where he died in exile.

MAY 21st

HEROD AGRIPPA I.   *Reading: Acts 12. 18-25.*

Like the other Herods this Agrippa combined a close friendship with the rulers at Rome with a slavish desire to ingratiate
himself with the Jews. Perhaps he imagined that it would be
easier to deal with the simple disciples than his uncle Antipas
had found it to deal with their Lord. If so he was wrong, for
the issue was essentially the same: he found himself in conflict
not with feeble men but with the mighty God. With his silver
robe still glinting in the sun and the insincere cheers of the
crowd still ringing in his ears, he was carried out of the
Caesarea theatre to pass five days of anguish before the same
gruesome death as had overtaken his grandfather, Herod the
Great, put an end to him also. The Church had prayed. God
had answered.

MAY 22nd

HEROD AGRIPPA II   *Reading: Acts 26. 19–32.*

The last of the Herods was as corrupt in morals as his predecessors had been, and so was Berenice. In mercy God gave
them a chance to hear the gospel. Agrippa's frivolous response
to Paul's powerful appeal might have set everybody laughing,
but for the courteous earnestness of the apostle's reply. Agrippa
did not profit from this encounter, but perhaps Paul did.
The king's influence confirmed Festus in his decision to send a
favourable recommendation to Rome. On his first hearing
Paul was acquitted. Nero would hardly think of condemning
to death a man who had been given a favourable report both
by the Roman Procurator and the Jewish puppet king. This
Herod was no murderer. Perhaps that is why he had a long
life and a tranquil death, having fled to Rome after the fall of
Jerusalem.

MAY 23rd

HEZEKIAH   *Reading: 2 Chronicles 30. 15–25.*

Hezekiah's problem was that false gods and idolatrous shrines
abounded everywhere. He knew that the Word of God
commanded the people to gather annually, so he sent out
invitations for the Passover that men might come to Jerusalem
to get right with God. Of course he was mocked by some,
but there were others ready to gather and seek God's pardon
and acceptance through sacrificial blood. In answer to prayer
their irregularities were overlooked and God met them and
they met Him. It was a time of much blessing and joy, so much
so that they stayed on for a further week of worship. Then away
they went home, and as they journeyed they destroyed the
idols and false altars. So Hezekiah's problem was solved, and
solved not by negative denunciations but by a positive exaltation of the Word and the will of God.

MAY 24th

HILKIAH   *Reading: 2 Kings 22. 3–13.*

To Hilkiah belonged the honour of restoring the Word of God to its place of authority among the people. For half a century there had been bitter persecution of true believers by the wicked king Manasseh, who had murdered men in their thousands and even had the godly old Isaiah cut in two, so it was said. The temple edifice had fallen into total disrepair and the books of the Law had completely disappeared. The Word of God was so unknown that the new king, Josiah, and Hilkiah the high priest had never seen a copy of it. Yet somehow, beneath all the rubble, a copy of the Law had been lying as if not so much buried as planted. Had this been the work of an unknown martyr for the faith? If so, the work was well done, for the harvest of righteousness and blessing came when Hilkiah and his men swept away the accumulated rubbish and brought it back to light again.

MAY 25th

HOBAB   *Reading: Numbers 10. 29–32.*

Originally Hobab had planned to go back home after visiting his brother-in-law, and even when he was invited to join the Israelites and share in their good things he still declined. Then Moses had the idea of asking him to help them with his expert knowledge of wilderness life. Hobab would not be expected to give them the route—that was decided by the Shekinah Cloud—but there was much help that an experienced nomad could give in smaller details. This idea of Moses' worked well. Hobab responded and took his family into the land (Judges 1. 16). People want to feel that they are needed, and the best way to encourage them is to ask for their help. When Moses said, "We will do you good", Hobab hesitated; but when he said, "Thou shalt be to us instead of eyes", he gladly accepted the invitation.

MAY 26th

HOPHNI   *Reading: 1 Samuel 2. 12–36*

"How long wilt thou be drunken? Put away thy wine from thee," old Eli had insultingly and unjustly exclaimed to Hannah. She was too respectful to do anything more than defend herself, but she might well have retorted that this was what he ought to have said to Hophni years before. Hannah, as she protested, was no child of Belial, but Hophni and his brother certainly were, and Eli had been all too slow to reprove them. What sort of a preacher is this, who denounces sin in his church and tolerates it in his home? He had, of course, been busy with his double task of ruler and priest. Perhaps he had not had time for young Hophni and his brother. but left them to their own devices while he was preoccupied with his religious work. Poor Hophni! He profited from his father's position, but he never came to know his father's God.

MAY 27th

HOSEA   *Reading: Hosea 11. 1–8.*

Since Hosea's domestic life was often used for spiritual illustrations, one wonders whether the expression "a cake not turned" (7. 8) arose from some disastrous cooking by his wife which resulted in an unpalatable substance burnt on one side and half-raw on the other. Hosea charged the people with being "half-baked" in their attitude to God, and warned them sternly of His displeasure. But although he threatened he also told them of God's great love for His erring people, the love that would not let them go. As he spoke he found his own heart filled with forgiving love for his unfaithful wife, Gomer. He knew that although she did not deserve it he must love patiently and not let her go either. So he bought her back from the slave market and gave her a place in his home, so showing that a man must practise what he preaches.

MAY 28th

HULDAH *Reading: 2 Kings 22. 12–20.*

We do not know if it was the wardrobe of the temple or of the royal palace which Huldah's husband kept, but in any case it is obvious that she was well known to the leading court officials, and what is more that she had a reputation among them for being a woman in touch with God. The high priest should really have been the man to help the king in the time of crisis occasioned by the finding of the book of the Law, but he and his companions found themselves quite unable to cope with the situation. Fortunately they remembered Huldah: only a woman maybe, but a woman with a reputation for a close walk with God. She was near at hand, so they tried her and discovered that her reputation was justified and that she did not fail them in their hour of need. She sent back to the king a message which was so balanced with true righteousness and true mercy that it was recognised as having come from God.

MAY 29th

HUSHAI *Readings: 2 Samuel 15. 30–37.*

Half way up the mount of Olives David gasped out a brief prayer about the traitor Ahitophel, a prayer which had no preliminaries and no formal ending. At the top of the hill he was met by his friend, Hushai the Archite, and realised that here was the answer to his prayer. So Hushai agreed to go over to Absalom to watch over David's interests in the rebel camp, and it was he who became the means of discrediting Ahitophel and of saving David. Some will ask why David had to plan in this way if he had already prayed. Others will approve his action but feel that his prayer was quite unnecessary. The truth is that prayer and practical prudence worked together. It is a pity that practical people tend to be prayerless, and that prayerful people are often so unpractical.

MAY 30th

ICHABOD   *Reading: 1 Samuel 4. 19–22.*

We would like to know more of the history of this tragic
orphan whose name Ichabod means "No glory". It was sad
enough to have lost mother, father and grandfather simul-
taneously on his birthday, but sadder still that his name and
the anniversary of his birth perpetuated the shameful loss of
the ark of God. We may hope that Samuel, being older, took
care to see that the growing lad was instructed in the thrilling
stories of how God watched over the sacred casket, of
Dagon's downfall, of the Philistines' fear and of the miraculous
way in which the cows left their calves to pull the cart on
which the ark was returned to Israel. Samuel never lived to see
it installed in its proper place in God's house, nor perhaps did
Ichabod, but in the end David brought it back. Ichabod was
not God's last word: the lost glory was restored.

MAY 31st

IMMANUEL   *Reading: Isaiah 7. 10–25.*

There can be no doubt that the true Immanuel is Jesus of
Nazareth, born of the virgin Mary. In Him the prophecy finds
its full and final expression. However, it is clear that there was
a historical child called Immanuel who was born in those
troubled days. We are not given details of this child's parent-
age; we only know that he was destined to grow up into a
world where all the past values had been thrown away, and
unfaithfulness to God's Word had brought its inevitable after-
math of decay and devastation. Ahaz's follies and infidelity
meant that Israel would lose its settled prosperity, leaving this
lad to come to adolescence when men were living as best they
could on the privation food of butter and honey. Well, even
if he had no material prospects, he had a marvellous name—
"God is with us". The sign may not have meant much to
Ahaz, but it means much to all true believers.

JUNE 1st

ISAAC   *Reading: Genesis 22. 1–12.*

Although Abraham had known from the first what a costly sacrifice was going to be offered on Mount Moriah, it was only gradually that Isaac learned of the great price which was to be asked of him there. Yet when the moment of truth came, although he was less prepared than Abraham and certainly much stronger physically, he made no resistance to his father, but submissively allowed himself to be bound and laid on the altar. The name Isaac means "laughter", which might have seemed ridiculous for one in such a position, yet proved true enough when God released him and restored him to share with his father the joy of those who have proved God's faithfulness. We only lose our laughter when we climb down from the altar ourselves instead of waiting for God to deliver us.

JUNE 2nd

ISAIAH (i)   *Reading: Isaiah 6. 1–8.*

Uzziah went to his place of worship in a wrong spirit. As a result he became a menace to others, had to be shut away, and was not even buried with the other kings. His relative, Isaiah, went to the same place of worship in a right spirit. He was so met by God that rich blessings flowed out from his life which continue to this day. The first effect of the vision which Isaiah had was to unnerve him, but he found that God had the answer to all his needs and was ready to use him. It was a transforming vision. Out of lips which had been defiled until God cleansed them came a flow of gracious prophecies, describing Christ in passages of ineffable beauty. Uzziah had a proud spirit and he became a menace. Isaiah was humbled and he became a blessing. It is striking that in the very same building two men of the same family could find such different destinies.

JUNE 3rd

ISAIAH (ii)   *Reading: Isaiah 39. 1–8.*

Whenever Hezekiah was in trouble he called for Isaiah, the man whose counsel and prayer support he greatly valued. But when his vanity was tickled by the Babylonian ambassadors and he was lured into folly, he kept the matter very quiet, so that Isaiah had to question him to know the truth. The prophet was aghast at discovering what had been going on behind his back, knowing that disaster would follow. A lesser man might have taken offence and given up. Isaiah, however, far from acting in this way, devoted the rest of his life to preparing God's people for the recovery which lay beyond their immediate distress. In doing so he gave us some of the most wonderful chapters of the whole Bible; he also showed himself to be a man of those rare virtues, patience and long-suffering.

JUNE 4th

ISCARIOT   *Reading: John 13. 18–32.*

Judas was called Iscariot because he came from the Judean town of Kerioth. Thus he was not a Galilean like most of the other apostles, and perhaps felt superior to them; yet his baseness was as black as that of any man in Bible history. His relationship to Christ, however, serves to accentuate the perfection of the Lord's character. Knowing him to be both thief and betrayer, Jesus yet exercised infinite patience and courtesy towards him, never letting the eleven know by any word or look of His that the man of Kerioth was a hypocrite. The Lord must have suffered greatly by reason of this relationship, but He never failed in His kindness. At the last supper He stooped to wash his feet and then, in a final gesture which yet failed to deter him, the Lord gave Judas the portion of honour. Even perfect love could do no more.

JUNE 5th

ISH-BOSHETH   *Reading: 2 Samuel 3. 1–11.*

Ish-bosheth inherited Saul's kingdom and seems also to have inherited his jealous and mistrustful nature. Suspiciousness is a habit which grows on a man; he begins with a real grievance, but broods until he begins to have imaginary grievances, suspecting an untruth in every statement and a conspiracy in every action. From suspecting one or two people he comes to regard even his closest companion with distrust. This is what Ish-bosheth did to Abner, the man who had refused to abandon him and had done his best to strengthen his crumbling regime. So warped in mind did Ish-bosheth become that he even accused Abner of an underhand plot to dethrone him. This was too much even for the faithful Abner, and the king soon found himself exposed to real traitors who murdered him in his bed. This was his end, and it was also the end of Saul's dynasty.

JUNE 6th

ISHMAEL   *Reading: Genesis 21. 8–21.*

Ishmael's name means "God hears", though it may seem that he was associated with unanswered prayer. To Abraham's request that Ishmael might be his spiritual successor God's answer was an emphatic "No". Yet Ishmael himself was miraculously preserved and blessed by God, finally being multiplied into a great nation with twelve princes as its rulers. It was true that the half-brothers could not live together, but at Abraham's death Ishmael and Isaac united to honour their father to whose prayers they both owed so much. It is quite wrong to complain that prayers are not answered just because it is not done in the way which the supplicant expected. God hears! Where true believers are concerned there is no such thing as unanswered prayer: Ishmael's story gives proof of this.

JUNE 7th

ISRAEL   *Reading: Genesis 32. 22–32.*

Normally men are given titles to celebrate their victories, but in spiritual matters it can be just the opposite. Jacob, for example, was made a prince as a result of his greatest defeat. He who had got the better of his father, his brother and his cousin, failed in his attempt to get the better of the mysterious Man who wrestled with him. The last desperate wrench which left him prostrate and permanently lamed was followed by the announcement of the replacement of his old name by the new and honoured title of Israel. To be defeated by God and to accept that defeat is the sure way of finding new dignity and power. The man whose native wit and natural strength have failed to obtain divine blessing may emerge from his exhaustion to find an entirely new life by complete dependence on God. Out of every new Jabbok there should emerge a new Israel.

JUNE 8th

ISSACHAR   *Reading: Genesis 49. 14–15.*

The prophecy concerning Issachar was that he would be so contented with his inheritance and find such rest in it that he would not hesitate to accept the burdens which it involved. This is always a scriptural idea, this harmony of rest and work. Issachar was to enjoy his inheritance by reason of his willingness to serve others and be governed by them. Too many Christians fail to find heart rest both in their daily work and in their church fellowship. Instead of being like Issachar, a willing ass submitting to the double load of burden-bearing, they are untamed asses, always discontentedly seeking new spheres and never prepared to bow their shoulders to a steady job. Christ invited men to take His yoke and promised that in this way they would enjoy true soul rest. As Issachar shows, such an attitude represents not weakness but strength.

JUNE 9th

ITHAMAR   *Reading: Numbers 4. 21–33.*

Ithamar was a priest of high office who was given the practical job of counting and checking the Tabernacle equipment: when the people of God were on the move it was particularly important that none of the cords or sockets or pins should be left behind in the sand. On the face of it this may not appear to be very priestly work, yet each hook for fastening the curtains, each socket of silver or brass, and even each tent peg and cord was essential for the proper functioning of the whole Tabernacle. The Kohathites who carried the sacred vessels needed no supervision, but, as the Gershonites and Merarites loaded up their waggons, the responsibility for seeing that not the least item was missing was entrusted to Ithamar. That a man of such high office should be chosen to do this reminds us that in the work of God even the details are important.

JUNE 10th

ITTAI   *Reading: 2 Samuel 15. 17–23.*

The adding of Ittai the Gittite to David's band of mighty men was perhaps a good feature of the otherwise sorry episode when David tried to become an ally of Achish, king of Gath (1 Samuel 27. 2). It was startling to find David fraternising with the uncircumcised enemies of the Lord, and the near disaster of Ziklag seemed to confirm the fears of those who anticipated calamity. Yet somehow, somewhere, this Philistine from Gath became so fired with the princely nobility of David that he himself became noble. Heedless of David's kindly dissuasion, Ittai, a foreigner recently arrived in Israel, claimed the privilege of devotedly sharing the dangers of his new king. So, now, it sometimes happens that one who has only recently been won to Christ puts more mature Christians to shame by his zeal and devotion.

JUNE 11th

JABEZ   *Reading: 1 Chronicles 4. 9–10.*

There are people whose lives are shadowed by a tendency to depression. Try as they may to throw it off, a certain heaviness of spirit comes constantly over them. Jabez was one of these. He inherited sorrow from his mother and carried this proneness to be gloomy all through his life, as is made evident by his name. He never changed that name, and he could not change his natural temperament. What marked him out as more honourable than his brothers, who had no such handicap, was his prayer that God would enlarge him in spite of what he was. This prayer was answered. God can do wonders for the man who faces his temperamental weaknesses instead of running away from them, and then trusts God to use them for the help of others. Jabez was saved from sorrow by being saved from himself.

JUNE 12th

JACOB   *Reading: Genesis 25. 19–34.*

Holiness cannot be inherited. Jacob had a saintly grandfather and a devout father, yet from his birth he was a treacherous deceiver. Isaac was not born until Abraham was a hundred years old and a mature man of God. When Isaac and Rebekah had their twins, Isaac was over sixty years old and had long walked with God. Surely the members of the third generation in such a succession should have been embodiments of holiness, but in fact they were two most unsatisfactory characters —Esau and Jacob. Clearly there is no evolutionary process in the realm of sanctification! When finally Jacob was transformed and fitted to take his place with his godly ancestors, Abraham and Isaac, it was not because he had inherited their holiness but because he had been sanctified by their God, and had learned to trust wholly in Him.

JUNE 13th

JAIRUS *Reading: Luke 8. 40–56.*

When Jairus's little daughter lay dying and Jesus had agreed to help, the crowd around them was so great that they moved at a snail's pace. But the patience of Jairus was to be tried still more, for when a sick woman touched Him Jesus stopped completely. There was the delay of the argument with Peter, the delay of finding the woman and listening to her shy explanation, and then the delay of Christ's reassuring words to her. They must have seemed intolerable delays to poor Jairus, who was finally made frantic by the report that the girl had died. It was then that Jesus turned to him and spoke the words which have been a comfort to so many tested believers— "Fear not; only believe." The delays of God are often hard to bear, but the subsequent joy which came to Jairus and his wife reminds us that although the Lord may seem to delay He is never late.

JUNE 14th

JAMES THE APOSTLE *Reading: Acts 12. 1–11.*

Peter, John and James were the three who formed Christ's special inner circle. They alone were with Him in Jairus's house, on the Transfiguration mount, and in Gethsemane. We know what fruitful ministries resulted in the case of the other two, but all that is recorded of James is that his life was prematurely cut off by Herod. Why did God allow this? Peter was delivered; why not James? Or why was so much trouble spent in preparing him for an apostolate which he never fulfilled? There is no answer to these questions, which apply equally to many other young servants of God who have died in their prime. At least in the case of James we have the satisfaction of knowing that his death pleased the Jews! This was a great compliment, and shows that he must have been a man with a vital testimony. What matters is not the number of years a man lives but how he lives them.

JUNE 15th

JAMES THE LORD'S BROTHER   *Reading: James 1. 2–25.*

In his letter James constantly reverts to the theme of the perfect man. No one was better qualified than he to write about human perfection, for he had lived all his early years in brotherly proximity to the Perfect Man. He had eaten at the same table with Jesus, slept in the same room and worked six days a week with Him in the same carpenter's shop. On the seventh day they had worshipped at the same synagogue. There were over three years of unhappy separation, but the resurrection brought James to his senses and to true faith. Then, as he reviewed those early years, he realised that he had been living as a brother with the only Man who has ever perfectly fulfilled the whole law of God. James had seen the perfect law of liberty in the home life of Jesus of Nazareth.

JUNE 16th

JEHOIADA   *Reading: 2 Chronicles 24. 1–16.*

Although Jehoiada was only priest and adviser to Joash he was given royal honours at his burial. This is even more striking when we find that the good king Joash was not buried in the same way. In those days a man's burial was an expression of the verdict of history on his life, and in the case of Jehoiada the whole nation was united in considering him to have been a king among men. He had lived a full life, taking over from his wife the task of preserving and educating their royal nephew, and under his influence worship was given a central place in the nation's life, so that men's wealth and their activities were devoted not to self but to God. The man who can live such a devoted life himself is a great man, but still greater the one who can influence others to do the same. Jehoiada was buried among the kings: no greater tribute had been paid to a man since God Himself buried Moses.

JUNE 17th

JEHORAM   *Reading: 2 Chronicles 21. 12–20.*

Jehoram died at the comparatively early age of forty. This in
itself was not necessarily a calamity, for an early death can
sometimes be accompanied by some comforting evidences
of God's kindness. He died after suffering for two years from
a painful wasting disease, but even so there have been believers
who have suffered and died in similar circumstances, and God
has got glory from their sufferings. Neither the early death
nor the two years of illness represented in itself a tragedy for
Jehoram: the tragedy was that he died unlamented. It was as
though at his death the epitaph read, "Here lies the body of a
man who was born to be a king, but who lived so self-
centred a life that at his death no one mourned him or felt that
now the world was a poorer place."

JUNE 18th

JEHOSHAPHAT   *Reading: 2 Chronicles 20. 13–26.*

The odds against king Jehoshaphat were so great that he and
his people could only stand before God in helpless appeal to
Him. They were told to move forward in faith, but this was
so hard that after consultation they agreed that they could
only advance if the singers were in the front, a decision which
would seem foolish to human judgment but which proved to
be right. It was praise of His Name which provoked God to
work for them: the enemies were so deceived that they fought
among themselves and indulged in such an orgy of self
destruction that there was nothing for Jehoshaphat to do but
gather up all the spoil. Thus the outcome proved that their
decision to make praise to God the basis of their advance was
absolutely sound. Jehoshaphat has passed on to all God's
people a spiritual principle—namely, that the only way to face
a battle is to "set the singers in front".

JUNE 19th

JEHOSHEBA   *Reading: 2 Kings 11. 1–3.*

It may sound like a fairy story to tell how the good aunt rescued the baby prince from his wicked grandmother, but what Aunt Jehosheba did for little Joash was solid and significant history. When she managed somehow to steal the baby away from the murderous hatred of Athaliah, she must have been puzzled to know where to hide him so that the idolatrous daughter of Jezebel would never come across him. The answer was ingeniously simple, so simple as to be inspired. She hid him in the house of the Lord, the one place which Athaliah had no desire at all to enter. So Jehosheba became the prototype of all those godly aunts who take their relationship seriously: by doing their utmost to surround little ones with an atmosphere of piety and prayer, they help to keep them protected from evil influences until they are able to take their place in the world.

JUNE 20th

JEHU   *Reading: 2 Kings 10. 28–36.*

This dynamic king was full of energy, and the work of God profited greatly from his tremendous zeal. The sad feature of his enthusiastic nature was that it expended its strength in negative efforts. It is true that all the condemnation spoken against the house of Ahab was carried out by Jehu: he drove his chariot furiously to the work, and he drew his bow with such strength that the arrow passed right through the wicked king. Then he went on to overthrow Jezebel and with fearful retribution trod her to death. "Come with me," he cried, "and see my zeal for the Lord." Up to this point Jehu's energy was well used for God, but it was all negative. When it came to positive obedience to the will of God for his own life and kingdom he was pathetically feeble. The life of faith must always be positive.

JUNE 21st

JEPHTHAH   *Reading: Judges 11. 29–40.*

Let the man who prides himself on his uncompromising consistency take care lest he carry it to such an extreme that it becomes stubborn folly. In a moment of deep anxiety Jephthah made this thoughtless vow which committed him to sacrificing his daughter. Seeing that he was a Spirit-filled deliverer many commentators have tried to excuse his action in proceeding with the sacrifice, but in fact his action was due to a misguided conception of his God, who would much rather have forgiven his rash promise. Jephthah was in the same class as King Saul who later made a similar vow, but in his case the people prevented him from killing his son, Jonathan (1 Samuel 14. 45), and clearly they were right. Jephthah and his poor daughter had no one to save them from their deluded folly. Jephthah's fear of inconsistency was not only unnecessary; it was tragic.

JUNE 22nd

JEREMIAH (i)   *Reading: Jeremiah 1. 1–12.*

When Jeremiah's ancestor, Aaron, was opposed by the tribal leaders God ordered the test of the rods to demonstrate His choice; Aaron's almond rod miraculously bore flowers and fruit, giving proof of his divine appointment, since resurrection life is God's prerogative. When the young Jeremiah was called to a task which was bound to attract public opposition he felt unable to obey, but he was re-assured by his vision of an almond rod; this reminded him of the familiar story of his great ancestor, Aaron, and made it plain that God's resurrection power is not a thing of the past but can be proved in present experience. His authority to speak for God was challenged over and over again, but he never gave up. He had seen the vision, and he was able to trust God that his ministry would not lack the authentic seal of resurrection life.

JUNE 23rd

JEREMIAH (ii)   *Reading: Jeremiah 20. 7–13.*

When a servant of God meets opposition not only from his enemies but also from his close friends, he at least expects some vindication from his God. There are times, however, when God gives no outward encouragement to His sorely tried servants, but seems rather to be letting them down. Jeremiah had his full share of such experiences, and felt so badly about it that he vowed never to speak for God again. He did not keep his vow, for he found the Word of God burning in his very bones. Since only God can kindle the inward fire it follows that in fact God was vindicating Jeremiah. It is true that the prophet saw little or no outward sign of vindication, which was why he almost gave way to despair; but, really, God was backing him up in the best possible way, by the inner fire of His Holy Spirit. So Jeremiah not only prophesied again: he burst out into spontaneous praise.

JUNE 24th

JETHRO   *Reading: Exodus 18. 17–27.*

We do not know if Jethro was a true believer before Moses came into his home in Midian, but it seems clear that by the time Israel were encamped on Mount Sinai Jethro was a convinced worshipper of the true God. He was not an Israelite, and only came to the camp on a brief visit, but, since an outsider sometimes has clearer judgment than those who are closely involved, he was able to give Moses some very necessary advice. Put into one word his advice was "delegate". He told Moses to draw in helpers, to encourage and commission others to take a share in the work, to resist the temptation to do it all himself just because he could do it best. This was excellent advice and fully justified Jethro's visit to the camp. Every man who is to be a successful leader must practise delegating tasks to others so that they can learn to take responsibility.

JUNE 25th

JOAB   *Reading: 1 Kings 2. 1–6.*

Joab was a man whose story would need many words for its telling. Indeed it would require two books, and when they were written they would seem to be biographies of entirely different men. One would tell of his superbly unselfish devotion to David, while the other would tell of his selfish ruthlessness in keeping his place as commander of David's armies. The first would be a story of courage and wisdom, the second one of vindictive treachery, for more than most men Joab had two different sides to his character. Only the grace of God can deliver a man from himself, and Joab does not seem to have known anything of that grace. So, in the list of David's mighty men, Joab's two brothers were honourably mentioned and even his armour-bearer was given a place, but significantly his name was omitted. A self-centred man can never achieve true greatness.

JUNE 26th

JOASH   *Reading: 2 Kings 12. 1–16.*

Joash claims attention as the inventor of the money-box. The principle of this kind of box with a hole in the lid is that once money has been inserted it cannot be withdrawn. It is particularly helpful for inducing children to save, but it is not only children who are tempted to take back what they have freely given. In Joash's day there was much misuse of the people's offerings until the king insisted that the freewill offerings should be placed in a chest: when it was full those authorised to do so were to unlock the box and allocate the money to the maintenance of God's house. Spiritual weakness can be caused by slackness in money matters, and God's people should be both generous and methodical in financial affairs, or they may find that the true riches are being withheld (Luke 16. 11).

JUNE 27th

JOB   *Reading: Job 42. 1–10.*

In the torrent of words which poured out from Job and his friends there were some real heart cries from Job which God duly noted and faithfully answered. Job longed that his words might be preserved in a book (19. 23), he wished that he knew where he could find God (23. 3), and he pined for past experiences of blessing (29. 2). God heard these requests and graciously granted them. Job did meet God for himself, he did have a full recovery of his earlier prosperity, and his words were written in the book which has brought comfort to countless sufferers since. God is always on the lookout for real heart cries, and is ready to ignore the many foolish questions and complaints which His children may make under pressure. He does not undertake to answer all our questions, but He does promise to answer all our prayers.

JUNE 28th

JOEL   *Reading: Joel 2. 23–32.*

We are sorry for those whose philosophy of life leaves no place for divine intervention, for it proves that they have no personal share in the great experience of Pentecost. Apart from the Incarnation this was God's greatest intervention in human affairs. Joel, who was greatly impressed by divine judgments and divine mercies, foresaw this break-through when he prophesied of the coming of God's Spirit to create a new body in which all barriers of birth, upbringing, sex and social standing would be set aside, and an entity formed in which His will would be done on earth as in heaven. It was a breathtaking idea, this new act of creation by the Holy Spirit bringing the Church to birth, but it was so wonderfully real to those who were present that they affirmed that this was what Joel had promised (Acts 2. 16). God made an entirely new beginning when the Holy Spirit brought the Church into being.

JUNE 29th

JOHN THE BAPTIST   *Reading: Luke 7. 18–34.*

There could be no greater suffering for an out-of-door type like John than to be shut up in a fortress prison. Those wilderness years were rough, but they were years of the Spirit's fulness; God was with him and he asked neither for riches nor for comfort, only for the privilege of being able to burn out for God. Instead of that he found himself in a living tomb, with no evidence of divine vindication. It is true that he had expressed his willingness to "decrease", but he had never thought that it would work out in this way. Finally he passed from the dungeon to the headsman's block. John the Baptist is surely an overwhelming argument for a future life. He had to finish this life without any kind of recompense for faithful and sacrificial service. There must be a reward in eternity for such a man. There must be—and there will be!

JUNE 30th

JOHN THE APOSTLE   *Reading: Revelation 1. 4–10.*

We notice that John was classed by the critics of his day as being among the "ignorant and unlearned" (Acts 4. 13), yet the fact remains that his Gospel is probably the most beautiful book ever written, and is certainly the most widely read. He was called a son of thunder by Christ Himself, and was keen at that time to call down fire on his enemies (Luke 9. 54), but he lived to write the noblest letter on love which has ever been penned or printed. Further, John began his life as a fisherman on a lake in the smallest of countries, yet before he died he had described vast cosmic events extending even beyond the limits of time. How can we explain this paradox of a man? Only by the fact that John had become possessed of a life infinitely larger and richer than his own; he was the embodiment of his great message that in Jesus Christ God has given His eternal life to men.

JULY 1st

JONAH   Reading: Jonah 4. 1–11.

In contrast with Jonah's pettiness we find in this book a revelation of the greatness of God, not only in the sphere of natural phenomena but also in the realm of merciful kindness. When he had been delivered from judgment by God's unmerited grace and permitted after all to be the messenger to Nineveh, Jonah should have been overjoyed at the remarkable success of his preaching there; but, far from this, he remained a narrow bigot, full of complaints and unable to share in God's pleasure at pardoning the undeserving. Centuries later, at the same port of Joppa, Peter faced a similar call, obeyed, and had thrilling success. Unlike Jonah, he rejoiced at God's outpoured mercy. Poor Jonah! It is an unhappy experience to try to limit to our own narrow circle the blessings of the God who loves the whole world.

JULY 2nd

JONATHAN   Reading: 2 Samuel 1. 17–27.

The brotherly love which existed between David and Jonathan was of an extremely high quality. It was sane and healthy, it was strong enough to stand all the stresses of Saul's divided kingdom, and it only ended with death. These were Old Testament men, but they put to shame many New Testament Christians who ought to excel in the matter of brotherly love. So often jealousies, friction and misunderstandings mar relationships, whereas David and Jonathan's love was not diminished at all by differences and temptations to rivalry. They began their relationship with mutual vows, continued it with mutual encouragement, and although circumstances forced them to be on opposing sides they never wavered in their mutual devotion. The brotherly love of David and Jonathan has become proverbial as something very special, but it should exist between Christians everywhere.

JULY 3rd

JOSEPH THE PATRIARCH   *Reading: Genesis 41. 38–45.*

For Joseph the day promised to be as wearisomely monotonous as ever. The only future which he could envisage was as bleak and cheerless as his prison cell. Then it happened! In no time he was promoted from prisoner to ruler, had exchanged his rough clothes for a gorgeous uniform, and was paraded through the streets in triumph. He had been snatched from the dungeon to the throne in a matter of hours. The Christian's hope is similar to Joseph's, though infinitely greater. Not in hours but in a moment he is to be snatched from this sordid world into the glory of Christ's presence. For him one day will begin as unpromisingly as all the others, but it will prove to be the day of his translation. All this will happen not by the decree of some earthly Pharaoh but by the word of the Lord (1 Thessalonians 4. 16). It may happen very soon.

JULY 4th

JOSEPH OF NAZARETH   *Reading: Matthew 1. 18–25.*

There is no need to think of Joseph as an elderly widower when he married Mary, but every reason for regarding him as a normal young man who was called to undertake a very abnormal responsibility. Perhaps he cannot rightly be called normal, for there are all too few young men who live in close fellowship with God as Joseph did. At every stage of his remarkable story he was guided by messages from God, and once the heavenly guidance had been given he obeyed without question or hesitation. He did delay in journeying down to Bethlehem, but as in this case the guidance only came through a government order he was not to be blamed, and by God's mercy he and Mary arrived there just in time. Joseph was no superman; he was a frail and fearful human being. But his faith and obedience made him a fit companion for the girl who had the supreme honour of being the mother of Jesus.

JULY 5th

JOSEPH OF ARIMATHAEA   *Reading: John 19. 38–42.*

A secret disciple is never a happy one. Joseph must have been heavy of heart when he carried that loved body from the Cross and buried it in his newly acquired tomb. It was now only a corpse which he could honour, and, like many another mourner, he must have grieved that it was now too late to declare his devotion to the One who had died. Miraculously for him it was not too late. His deep sorrow gave place to joy when he found that his Lord had risen from the dead. Joseph must have been one of the boldest to testify after Pentecost, and one of the most ready to share his wealth with others as a token of his great love for Christ. No more secret discipleship for him!

JULY 6th

JOSHUA THE WARRIOR   *Reading: Exodus 17. 8–16.*

Joshua was destined to be field commander of Israel's forces, and his education was in the hands of God, who alone knew his future and the campaigns in which he would be engaged. This first clash with Amalek proved that his army could be victorious, but the outcome did not depend so much on Joshua as on the invisible intercessor who lifted up the rod of God on his behalf. The Lord was concerned that Joshua should realise the importance of this basic lesson, and had it written in a book by Moses. So one of the greatest of all commanders began his military education with the fundamental principle that all battles are decided in the unseen before their results become evident. The brilliant success of his conquest of Canaan shows how well he learned the lesson, and reminds us that in the spiritual warfare this is still the secret of victory.

JULY 7th

JOSHUA THE PRIEST   *Reading: Zechariah 3. 1–10.*

Joshua's predicament had the nightmare quality of some of the most worrying dreams: he had on the right clothes, but they were in a filthy state; he was in the inner sanctuary, but with his priestly garments in a soiled condition. This signified that he and the people whom he represented were sinners in the sight of God and unfit for His presence. Satan was loud in his accusations, whereas Joshua was silent and ashamed. God, however, was not silent. He spoke words of grace which brought about the removal of the defilement, and provided beautiful clothes so that the redeemed sinner could be at ease in His presence. This reversal, too, may seem like a dream, but justification is no dream; it is the act of God's grace whereby He does for the contrite sinner just what He did for Joshua. In this way the accuser is silenced for ever.

JULY 8th

JOSIAH   *Reading: 2 Chronicles 34. 22–33.*

In those dark and shameful days which preceded Judah's captivity, Josiah stands out with as brilliant a light as any of his predecessors. When he came to the throne the complete overthrow of Jerusalem was inevitable, though he himself was promised security. So here he was, in the twilight of his age, safe himself but powerless to avert the coming judgment. It would have been easy to have drifted smugly along, happy in his own security and careless about the doomed society in which he lived. Instead of doing this he made energetic efforts to honour God and to give an inspiring lead to the people to do the same. It might have been argued that the spiritual situation had deteriorated beyond recovery, but even if this were true it would not have excused Josiah from doing his best. In any case he was taking no chances, and nor should we.

JULY 9th

JUDAS THADDAEUS *Reading: John 14. 19–24.*

This Judas was "not Iscariot" in name and "not Iscariot" in nature either. We have no detailed description of him, but this one recorded utterance which is given us shows that his supreme desire was not for anything earthly, but for a deeper knowledge of his heavenly Lord. The world knows (or at least can know) the historical facts about Jesus. They are not without importance, but this spiritually minded apostle wanted something more than that: he asked for guidance as to how a man can obtain an inner appreciation of the true character of Christ Jesus. The answer which he received gave promise of the miracle of the indwelling Spirit. Judas the traitor shows us that this world's goods can never satisfy. This Judas shows us what does bring deep heart satisfaction—namely, a living experience of the love of God.

JULY 10th

KOHATH *Reading: Numbers 4. 1–20.*

The most privileged branch of Levi's family were the men who carried the ark and the sacred vessels of the Lord's house. This they had to do by hand, as no waggons were allocated to them. The most striking thing about their service was that they were never allowed to see the articles which they carried, nor even to touch them. The Gershonites and the Merarites had the pleasure of seeing and displaying the bright colours and the gleaming metals of their burdens. The men of Kohath had literally to walk by faith and not by sight, for the holy furniture was covered by Aaron and his sons. Nobody could prove to the sons of Kohath that their loads were sacred or valuable. All that they knew was that their High Priest had allotted "every man to his service and to his burden", and that their privilege was to offer their shoulders unquestioningly for their God-given tasks.

JULY 11th

KORAH   *Reading: Numbers 26. 9–11.*

Those who are scandalised by the second commandment's reference to the visiting of the iniquity of the fathers upon the children should consider the experience of Korah's sons. Korah himself led an uprising against the authorities and met disaster at the hands of God. The original story gives the impression that, as with Dathan and Abiram his fellow conspirators, the entire family was swallowed up alive, but the truth is that Korah's sons were spared, and in fact they later had an honoured part in the temple worship and gave their name to some psalms. So the rest of the second commandment was the really effective part, ". . . showing mercy unto thousands . . .". Presumably Korah's sons disassociated themselves from their father's attitude, and were spared and blessed by the God who delights in mercy and is only jealous for men's good.

JULY 12th

LABAN   *Reading: Genesis 31. 36–55.*

Laban's idea of blessing was hard cash, as may be seen from his eager welcome to Abraham's servant who had given expensive jewellery to his sister, Rebekah (Genesis 24. 30–31). When he was much older Rebekah's son, Jacob, came to him for help, and he grasped eagerly at the profit which he could extract from Jacob's predicament and from the love which he felt for Rachel. All the tendencies of Laban's youth had hardened into sharp greed, and, what was worse, he did not hesitate to use pious phrases to cloak his covetousness. His main usefulness in life seems to have been to provide a mirror in which Jacob could see his own faults. Jacob's indignation at the sight of his own character reflected in the behaviour of Laban helped him towards deliverance from himself. Sometimes the person of whom we so disapprove is merely reflecting our own faults.

JULY 13th

LAMECH   *Reading: Genesis 4. 16–24.*

Enoch, the seventh from Adam on Seth's side, was the man who walked humbly with his God. Lamech, seventh from Adam on Cain's side, went his own way and was confident that he could manage his own affairs. When his son learned to make sharp metal weapons he began to base his confidence on armaments. Whether he was telling his wives what he had already done to the young aggressor, or whether he was voicing a threat as to what he would do, it is clear that he now felt he was in a position to inflict savage retribution on any who dared attack him. Cain had needed God to protect him; Lamech felt well able to look after himself. This world's weapon is revenge: Christ's weapon is forgiveness. In both cases they have no limits but are to "seventy times seven" (Matthew 18. 22).

JULY 14th

LAZARUS THE BEGGAR   *Reading: Luke 16. 19–31.*

This name is the latinised form of Eliezar, which means "God is my help". When the Lord Jesus told this story He may have chosen the name to imply that the sick beggar was in fact a man of faith. While Lazarus lived he had none to care for him, and when he died none to bury him, but he found rich consolation in the life beyond. Let there be no mistake about it, this is a moral universe. Nobody can live to self in callous disregard of the sufferings of others, and pass on to a hereafter of blissful forgetfulness. And certainly no one can truly claim God as his help without proving that the sufferings of this present time are not worthy to be compared with the glory which is to be revealed. Happy is the poorest man if he has God to be his help.

JULY 15th

LAZARUS THE LOVED. *Reading: John 11. 21–44.*

Why did Christ shed tears over Lazarus? Was it at the reminder of how death has marred this beautiful world which He had been instrumental in creating? Man was not made for tears, but tears have been his lot ever since he turned his back on God. No wonder that the Creator Himself wept! Or was it because of the sorrow which had come to the Bethany household? Although their sorrow was soon to be turned into joy, the fact remains that for them the way to glory was by pain and tears. Was it perhaps that He wept in sympathy with them? Or was it, as some have thought, that He wept at bringing Lazarus back from the bliss of paradise to this troubled world? We are foolish enough to wish that our blessed dead could return to us here on earth. Is it possible that the prospect of such a return for Lazarus filled the heart of Christ with sorrow?

JULY 16th

LEAH *Reading: Genesis 29. 16–35.*

Leah's younger sister was strikingly beautiful, but she herself was unattractive, her chief defect being that her eyes were "tender", that is weak or delicate. This was more than physical, for she was one of those shortsighted women who try to force a man to love her. She began with a subterfuge, planned indeed by her unscrupulous father, but to which she must have been a willing partner. How can any man love a woman who has captured him by a trick, especially if he cares for someone else, as Jacob did? Leah managed to get herself a husband, and she bore him quite a number of children, but she never succeeded in winning Jacob's love. With the birth of each son she said that "this time" it would be different, but it never was. Human love can never be demanded; it must always be won.

JULY 17th

LEMUEL *Reading: Proverbs 31. 1–9.*

His mother's advice was meant to urge Lemuel to live worthily of his kingly vocation. Alcohol, according to her, was not fitting for a man with such a title: if less fortunate men who have none but themselves to consider want to find comfort in strong drink, then let them do so; but a man who is called to set a high example to others and to spend his life in devoted service on their behalf should count it a privilege to be an abstainer. It is not difficult to argue from Scripture that alcohol, as such, is not forbidden to Christians, whose life in any case is not subject to rules and regulations. If, however, we desire to live worthily of our high calling in Christ we shall be reminded, as Lemuel was, that there are some things which are "not for kings". The royal mother felt that alcohol was one of a number of unseemly things.

JULY 18th

LEVI *Reading: Luke 5. 27–31.*

This New Testament descendant of the famous priestly family of Levi was usually called Matthew. He alone tells us that he was a tax collector, but Luke tells us much about him that he was too modest to mention in his own Gospel. One was that he was rich, for the reception he gave was a lavish one. Another was that he had readily given up all his wealth to follow Christ. It is instructive to note the order in which Luke records his actions—he first "forsook all", and then he "rose up". This shows that something revolutionary had taken place in his heart before it revealed itself in his action. It is a common mistake to try to follow Christ while inward matters of renunciation and committal are still half undecided. Those who lack Levi's firm decision will probably miss much of the overflowing joy which marked his farewell feast to his friends.

JULY 19th

LOIS   *Reading: 2 Timothy 1. 2–5.*

Paul owed much to a grandmother—not his, but Timothy's.
Lois was a woman with a vital faith which was rooted in a
deep knowledge and love of the Scriptures. She had taken
care that her daughter, Eunice, had been well instructed in the
Word of God and, even if she did not approve of her Gentile
son-in-law, she took the same care with their son, Timothy.
His father's unconcern for spiritual things may have given her
an even greater interest in her delicate and sensitive grandson.
If she lived long enough to witness the devoted service which
Timothy gave to Paul and to the gospel, she must have felt
amply rewarded. In any case, her name has come down to
posterity as an eminently successful grandmother. This may
not sound a very heroic role, but it can be of immeasurable
importance.

JULY 20th

LOT   *Reading: Genesis 19. 12–29.*

We are told in the New Testament that Lot was righteous,
but we are also told that he was an unhappy man. This sounds
like a contradiction, but the cause of his unhappiness is not
hard to discover: it was his love of the world. At first he was
content to admire the view of Sodom, but later he moved into
the city itself. With the calamity of war he was captured with
its people, and was only released by the kindness and courage
of his uncle Abraham. Far from learning his lesson and moving
out of that wicked city, he returned to its permissive atmosphere and even became a figure of importance there. Once
again Abraham came to his rescue, and by his persistent prayer
ensured the rescue of Lot before Sodom was overwhelmed in
judgment. Those who wish to know what Paul meant by
being saved "so as by fire" should consider the fate of Lot.

JULY 21st

LUKE   *Reading: Colossians 4. 6–14.*

It has been said that a minister sees people at their best, a lawyer sees people at their worst, while a doctor sees people as they really are. This friend and companion of Paul wrote two books about people as they really were, his Gospel and the Acts. He shows us saints like Zachariah, Stephen and Barnabas. He shows us sinners like Zacchaeus, the dying thief and Saul of Tarsus. He discloses the weakness as well as the virtues of the early Christians. Above all he gives a true picture of the perfect Son of Man, both on earth and operating from His place in glory. The only man of whom he says nothing at all is himself, but that is typical of a good doctor. Like many other doctors, too, Luke had a favourite prescription. It was prayer. It should be taken as required, being a certain remedy for all ills.

JULY 22nd

LYDIA   *Reading: Acts 16. 11–15.*

The first convert to Christ in the continent of Europe was a business woman called Lydia. To Paul, who was searching for a "man of Macedonia", she may have seemed of secondary importance. If so he was mistaken, for Lydia's home became the first centre of worship and witness in our continent; the first European night of prayer was held in that home, and God was moved to send a literal earthquake to shake the prison and a spiritual earthquake to convict the jailor. Luke stayed on there after Paul and Silas had left, and from these simple beginnings in the house of Lydia there emerged a church which was a credit to Paul and a joy to God. All these things show what God can do with a business woman who gets truly converted, whether in the first century or in the twentieth.

JULY 23rd

MALACHI   *Reading: Malachi 3. 6–12.*

No wonder that the believers of Malachi's day were full of complaints and troubles! How could they expect prosperity when they were depriving God of His rights? They thought that tithing was a thing of the past; it sounded nice in religious history, but they did not think that it was practical in their day. It is always practical and it is always open to proof. "Put God to the proof," urged Malachi, "and do it now. Give honestly, give gladly, give freely to God, and the very windows of heaven will open to you in overflowing blessing." With this challenge from Malachi the Old Testament closes. The New Testament records how the whole tithe was brought in, first by the Lord Jesus and then by His people, and there can be no doubt that the windows of heaven were wide open for them in those early days of Christianity.

JULY 24th

MALCHUS   *Reading: Luke 22. 47–53.*

The servant's name was Malchus (John 18. 10). We might be tempted to feel pleased that at least one of that brutal group should feel the sharp edge of a sword. It was little enough—just to lose an ear! Luke the physician, however, would not agree, and took careful note of what followed. In spite of the fact that His mind must have been occupied with many weightier matters, Christ, the great Physician, insisted on touching and healing the wound before allowing Himself to be hurried away to condemnation and crucifixion. So the last miracle performed by our Lord at the end of a ministry of miracles was an act of kindness to one of His persecutors. If this could not melt the heart of Malchus then nothing could.

JULY 25th

MANASSEH THE PATRIARCH *Reading: Genesis 48. 12–20.*

Joseph called his first son Manasseh ("forgetting") because he had been enabled by God to forget the hardships and injustices of the past. Having recorded this fact, he expressed his appreciation of God's subsequent blessing in the name of his second son Ephraim ("fruitfulness"). God then reversed the order, as, against Joseph's wishes but under divine urge, Jacob made it his supreme act of faith to insist that Ephraim must be given the first place. The important fact to emphasise was not the suffering but the fruitfulness. This is equally true today. The very effort of "forgetting" may be negative, giving us the opportunity to dwell on our past trials and the injustices which we have suffered. First place must rather be given to praise, to the appreciation of the positive values which have come to us and to others.

JULY 26th

MANASSEH THE KING *Reading: 2 Chronicles 33. 9–16.*

The Bible is an unexpected book. Manasseh was the worst kind of totalitarian monster. He mercilessly persecuted innocent men; he did his utmost to suppress all faith and virtue; he dragged the nation into vile corruption. He did this for many years and was the direct cause of Judah's captivity. Then at the climax of his just retribution, God had mercy on him as he cried out in repentance. The moralist may find such a last-minute repentance repugnant, because he is not able to appreciate the greatness of God's grace, but such magnanimity is undoubtedly God-like. Manasseh's story should encourage us to hope that members of our family whose present conduct and attitude cause us so much distress may yet be reconciled to God, even at the eleventh hour. We must not give up hoping and praying.

JULY 27th

MANOAH   *Reading: Judges 13. 10–23.*

If ever you are plunged into gloom by the unwholesome happenings described in the book of Judges, then turn to these verses and read again the story of the godly simplicity of Manoah. See him listening attentively to his excellent wife, never questioning God's message but only praying for repeated and more explicit instructions; notice how implicitly he believed God's promises and desired to honour His messenger; listen to his humble fear that perhaps he had come too close to God, and to the quiet re-assurance of his trustful wife. As you read you will find yourself thanking God that there was still sweetness and purity in that corrupt age, and perhaps you will feel urged to pray that in our own age there may be modern Manoahs, whose simple piety may contrast with the surrounding lawlessness.

JULY 28th

MARK   *Reading: Mark 14. 35–42.*

Where did the Gethsemane narrative come from if the disciples were all asleep? These verses suggest that Mark himself was a silent witness, standing in awe under the shadow of the trees. The moving scene bears the marks of an eye witness account, even to the recording of the Aramaic word for Father. He may have risen hurriedly from his bed to follow the apostolic band from his mother's upper room; later, when the soldiers tried to catch him, he may have left his sheet in their hands and run home to safety. He would not be likely to forget so poignant a lesson on the costliness of obedience to the Father's will. Mark himself had many spiritual ups and downs before he was prepared to accept the full will of God in his own life. When he eventually came to that place of victory it was because he allowed the Spirit of Christ to have full sway in his heart, so that he himself could say, "Abba, Father."

JULY 29th

MARTHA   *Reading: Luke 10. 38–42.*

Jesus loved Martha. He did not try to make her the same as her sister Mary; He loved her just as she was. This does not mean that He did not correct her; He always corrects the people whom He loves. On the last occasion when Christ had a meal at Bethany it was again prepared by Martha, a silent Martha this time, but a no less efficient one. It might have made a pretty story if on this last occasion the evangelist had depicted her as sitting at the Lord's feet, or even anointing them, but it would neither have been true to life nor have conveyed the right lesson to his readers. God's revelation shows that Martha became a more sanctified woman, but still a serving woman, dedicated to domesticity. This is how He wanted her, and this is how He loved her.

JULY 30th

MARY OF NAZARETH   *Reading: Luke 2. 39–49.*

Some might think it unsuitable that the virgin mother should be included in this account of ordinary mortals. They would be wrong, for she—like the rest of us—was ready to admit her own need of a Saviour. Of course she was greatly blessed. "Blessed art thou among women," Gabriel told her; Elisabeth repeated this and added, "Blessed is she that believeth"; while Mary herself was confident that future generations would call her so. A pious woman once interrupted the Lord Jesus with the exclamation, "Blessed is the womb that bare thee, and the breast which thou didst suck", only to receive from Him the swift and illuminating retort, "Yea rather, blessed are they that hear the Word of God, and keep it" (Luke 11. 27–28). In that respect also, Mary was blessed and glad to share her blessing with all the other believers.

JULY 31st

MARY OF MAGDALA   *Reading: Mark 16. 1–11.*

Why was this Mary the first to be spoken to by the Lord after
His resurrection? Was it because she was the most devoted?
Had her deliverance from demons filled her with a special
kind of love which qualified her for this honour? Was it not
rather because she was the most needy of them all? She might
well have been fearful that the seven unclean spirits were
capable of repossessing her now that the Lord was no longer
alive. Despair is dangerous for us all: for her it might well
have been fatal. As much as any she needed to know the
reality and significance of the resurrection. Her Lord was alive
and near; by His ascension He would come even nearer, and
never fail to maintain the effectiveness of her deliverance from
evil powers. The indwelling of the Holy Spirit is the surest
safeguard against demon possession.

AUGUST 1st

MARY OF BETHANY   *Reading: John 12. 1–8.*

Mary's action in anointing Christ for His burial suggests that
she truly understood something of the nature of His death and
even His resurrection. The others had probably heard the same
truths that she listened to as she sat at the feet of Jesus, and with
her they had witnessed the raising from the dead of her
brother Lazarus. They had heard and seen, but they had not
understood. Mary was different from them, not because she
had had more instruction but probably because she had more
sacrificial love. Such love is perceptive and sensitive. Mary
could not have explained the atoning death of Christ nor
clearly foreseen the manner of His resurrection, but she could
sense them both. Her love was not only sensitive; it was
wonderfully comforting. Mary did more than anoint Christ's
body: she provided balm for His soul.

AUGUST 2nd

MARY OF JERUSALEM   *Reading: Acts 12. 10–17.*

It was not a chance wind which blew open the iron gate of the Jerusalem prison but a terrific stream of energy which proceeded from Mary's home prayer meeting. Peter was so bewildered by the amazing happening that he wondered if it were all a dream, but when he was certain that he was in the realm of sober realities he knew where the earthly source of the energy would be located, and made his way directly to Mary's house. Instinctively he turned to that house, and his instinct was right. The church which was standing behind him had no special building, no officials, and no order of service; but it had effective power. Mary was the kind of woman who could be trusted to open her home for prayer when God's servants were in trouble, as many others have since done. There could only be one Mary of Nazareth, but there have been many Marys like the one in Jerusalem.

AUGUST 3rd

MATTHEW   *Reading: Matthew 10. 1–7.*

God needs preachers: He also needs writers. Matthew's profession as a tax collector meant that he was a man of a methodical mind who was accustomed to keeping records. So far as he was concerned his response to Christ meant that when he became a disciple he left everything, including this facility, but God chose that his pen was not to be abandoned but to be sanctified. If Paul could claim that he had been set apart from birth, surely the same must have been true of Matthew, who was given his ability as a writer to make sure that the teachings of Christ were recorded verbatim. Our God-given natural qualities can be used either for evil or for good. At first Matthew used his pen in the service of money making, but later he used it to record the Sermon on the Mount and much more of Christ's teaching. Whether he ever preached or not, he certainly provided a wealth of sermon material for those who do; his tongue was the pen of a ready writer.

AUGUST 4th

MATTHIAS   *Reading: Acts 1. 15–26.*

"The lot is cast into the lap, but the whole disposing thereof is of the Lord." Matthias had abundant reason to be thankful that his position in the apostolic band was so firmly based on Scripture. In those pre-Pentecost days they had no other way of coming to their final decisions. Their reasoning had produced two men as alternatives, but, being aware that human reasoning has its limitations, they then turned to prayer and asked the Lord, who alone knows men's hearts, to decide the matter for them. We have no need to cast lots now. The sad thing is that we often act as though we had no need for heavenly guidance. Our selection committees tend to discuss the pros and cons and then to accept a majority vote, or else perhaps to compromise by choosing both men in order to avoid bad feeling. We are post-Pentecost and have the Holy Spirit as our guide.

AUGUST 5th

MELCHIZEDEK   *Reading: Genesis 14. 17–24.*

Who was this mysterious king-priest? Nobody knows. What we do know and appreciate was his reception of Abram when the man of God came home flushed with victory. Our moments of success are our moments of greatest peril. Abram was about to be met by the king of Sodom who would have given him the things which were calculated to weaken his friendship with God. By a timely intervention, however, Melchizedek interposed himself between the king and Abram, causing the latter to pause for a while and sit down to a symbolic meal of bread and wine. This he needed for physical refreshment, but much more to remind him of his complete dependence on God. In this way he was saved from compromise and fortified to reject the world's attractions; he was not interested in material advantages when he had tasted the satisfying fulness of God's love. One of the purposes of the Lord's table is to strengthen believers to resist this world's blandishments.

AUGUST 6th

MEPHIBOSHETH   *Reading: 2 Samuel 9. 1–13.*

Mephibosheth was a feeble survivor of a distinguished but ruined family, seeking refuge in obscurity and anonymity. David, however, searched him out and summoned him to Jerusalem. If Mephibosheth went in fear, his fear was soon allayed, for he was promised a restored heritage and given a place of honour among the royal princes. As he sat continually at David's table none could distinguish him from the king's sons; true, he was lame on both his feet, but this deformity was mercifully hidden by the table. Here he was, raised from obscurity to a place of honour "for Jonathan's sake"! And here are we, our lameness not hidden but healed, seated at the table of God's grace, and all for the sake of the Lord Jesus.

AUGUST 7th

METHUSELAH   *Reading: Genesis 5. 21–27.*

Methuselah never knew a father who was out of step with God, for it was at his birth that his father, Enoch, began to walk with God. Perhaps Enoch was so profoundly moved with wonder at this new little life committed to his care and so deeply aware of his great responsibility in becoming a father, that he was driven to seek a closer walk with the Lord. Many other fathers have felt the same at the birth of their firstborn, but have failed to keep the vows they then made. Enoch never faltered, so that when Methuselah grew up and had a son of his own, his father Enoch was still maintaining his close communion with the Almighty. He passed from this earth to even closer communion, but Methuselah lived on. He lived on until he became the oldest man that history has ever known, but we are not told if he ever learned to walk with God.

AUGUST 8th

MICAH   *Reading: Micah 5. 1–4.*

Micah's claim to have been full of power by the Spirit of the Lord may be justified by his accurate prophecy concerning the ploughing up of Zion (3. 12). This unlikely prediction was literally fulfilled in A.D. 70 when the Romans were so convinced that treasure had been secreted in Jerusalem that, under their acting commander Terentius Rufus, they actually tore up the ground, exposing sewers and aqueducts, and used a ploughshare on the foundations of the temple. Yet a much less sensational prophecy is the one with which Micah is always associated: the whole Christian world knows that it was he who foretold deliverance and peace by the birth of the divine eternal Ruler in the humble town of Bethlehem. Both prophecies were true; both were given by the power of the Spirit; but the Jews who refused the message of Bethlehem had to face the horrors of the ploughshare.

AUGUST 9th

MICAIAH   *Reading: 1 Kings 22. 26–35.*

Micaiah stood alone among all the false prophets and told Ahab the unpalatable truth, even though he was put in prison and threatened with death. In spite of all his threats Ahab was afraid of the message, and took elaborate precautions to avoid its fulfilment. But there is no armour against God. The death-dealing arrow was fired at random by some careless Syrian soldier who could not bother to aim at a target, but it flew straight to the one vulnerable spot in the armour of the one man who mattered. No doubt the false prophets excused their erroneous forecasts, as false prophets always do. Micaiah did not need to excuse or justify himself, for he was fully vindicated by events. The man who keeps faithful to God's Word may have to stand alone for a time, but in the end he will be vindicated.

AUGUST 10th

MICHAL   *Reading: 2 Samuel 6. 14–22.*

Michal made the mistake of imagining that dignity prohibits the display of emotion, demanding a constant pose of superiority in order to enforce respect. To her the sight of David, dancing enthusiastically with the joy of heaven in his heart, was despicable. She did not even have the self-restraint to keep her thoughts to herself, but rushed out to meet her royal husband loudly voicing her sneering contempt. She did more harm to herself than to David, for he was well able to maintain his kingly dignity before the people, who respected him all the more for his unpretentious spontaneity. Poor Michal! She was so anxious to maintain her position as a queen; but she behaved more like a brawling peasant woman, concerned with what other people thought rather than with the praises of the Lord.

AUGUST 11th

MIRIAM   *Reading: Numbers 12. 1–15.*

Miriam could never forget that she was Moses' big sister. When he became the great leader of Israel she enjoyed a privileged position among all the nation's women. Then Moses chose the wrong wife—at least, that was what Miriam thought; but of course to jealous eyes all rivals are wrong. She was not really concerned for Moses or for Aaron, but she was unwilling for any other woman to occupy the place which until then had belonged to her. This jealous spirit brought trouble and delay to the whole divine enterprise, since no further progress could be made until Miriam was cleansed from her leprous state. There are many causes of weakness and breakdown in the work of God, but it is surprising how often the real cause of the trouble is jealousy. Not much progress is possible until that leprous condition is recognised and cleansed.

AUGUST 12th

MISHAEL   *Reading: Daniel 3. 23–29.*

Mishael's name was a testimony to the uniqueness of God, so it is not surprising that the Babylonians changed it to Meshach. On no occasion does it appear alone but is always flanked by Hananiah (Shadrach) on one side and Azariah (Abed-nego) on the other. Happy is the man who has two such reliable companions as Mishael had. The three trained together, and learned to pray together. Then they had to face the world together, and because they remained true to God they had to enter the fire together. In that terrible furnace they walked together in their unique fellowship with God, and together they proved that He is nearer to His servants in fiery trials than He is anywhere else. When they emerged unharmed they were still together, and their companionship reached its climax when it gave a new title to God—"the God of Shadrach, Meshach and Abed-nego."

AUGUST 13th

MOSES THE BABY   *Reading: Exodus 2. 1–10.*

The first recorded act of Moses was to cry. It was all he could do; the rest had to be done by his family. The parents worked together, collecting the bulrushes, weaving the basket and waterproofing it with pitch. Miriam too played her part, young though she was. In that way a believing family launched their new baby on to the threatening waters of that heathen land; and in that way believing parents can introduce their infants to the still more perilous waters of our modern society. Our bulrushes are prayers, woven into an ark of protection for the little life; our pitch is love which makes a safe covering; and our confidence, like that of Moses' family, is in the sovereign power of God who works for those who trust in Him. He even used Moses' cry to touch the heart of Pharaoh's daughter: all things are His servants.

AUGUST 14th

MOSES THE PRINCE *Reading: Hebrews 11. 24–28.*

It is clear that Moses made good use of the first-class education his privileged position enabled him to receive (Acts 7. 22). This shows what a crisis it must have been when he decided to sacrifice his whole career for the sake of his fellow Israelites. Nobody will suggest that he acted very wisely when he killed the Egyptian: on the contrary, it is easy to criticise his rash violence. Yet how many of us in his position would have been willing to step down from a princedom to slavery in order to bring God's help to fellow slaves? There was something Christlike in his renunciation. It failed, because Christlike acts demand a Christlike character, and this Moses did not have—not yet! From this moment, however, God's hand came on him in a new way in order to give him that character. There is no need to worry unduly about being unwise or too impulsive: God will undertake to sanctify you if you dedicate yourself to Him and His service.

AUGUST 15th

MOSES THE SHEPHERD *Reading: Exodus 3. 1–10.*

While Moses was a prince he attempted to lead God's people, using the methods he had learned in the schools of Egypt, those of domineering violence. He failed, as every spiritual leader will fail who uses such methods. So Moses had to be taught lessons of patience which only the shepherd life could teach him, and Moses the prince was changed into Moses the shepherd, a very different person. He had endured forty years of discipline in the wilderness where he learned patience, gentleness and tender compassion, and these were the qualities which enabled God to entrust him with his new commission. In himself he now felt most inadequate, but this also was a necessary part of his training. It was his shepherd's rod which became the symbol and the secret of God's power.

AUGUST 16th

MOSES THE LAWGIVER   *Reading: Exodus 34. 29-35.*

God Himself gave the law to Moses, and time has shown that it cannot be improved upon. Moses, however, broke the original tablets as soon as he had received them, in his anger at the people's sin: they had already broken the law, which in fact set a standard which was impossibly high for man. Later he received a re-writing of the same law, and these second tablets were never broken, but were preserved intact in the ark of God. So the lawgiver (who himself could not keep the law) received an indication that there would come a perfect Man capable of fulfilling it in the letter and in the spirit. No wonder that Moses' face shone when he came down from the mountain with such a revelation! He had enjoyed a pre-vision of Christ. The believer who keeps in view the perfection of the Saviour will also be radiant, for Christ has perfectly fulfilled the law for him.

AUGUST 17th

MOSES THE INTERCESSOR   *Reading: Exodus 32. 31-34.*

How many of us would pour out our hearts in compassionate prayer for people who had failed us as grievously as Aaron and Israel had failed Moses? Moses seems to have grasped the principle of atonement, and to have realised that Israel's enormous sin could never be forgiven by the offering of sacrificial animals. He therefore made the proposal that if the people could not be pardoned on any other basis God would accept him as a sacrifice, taking away their sins by blotting him out of God's book. The offer was not accepted, for only Christ can bear the sins of others, but it shows us the price that Moses was prepared to pay as an intercessor. The value of our prayers will be assessed not by their length or language but by this same criterion of selfless compassion for others, even those who have wronged us.

AUGUST 18th

MOSES THE FAILURE   *Reading: Numbers 20. 1–13.*

Self-assertion in the service of God robbed Moses of the supreme prize which he had so desired. One of the most striking features of this sad breakdown in his spiritual career was that it coincided with one of his greatest miracles. The man who silenced the complaints of the people, and apparently delivered them from death by producing torrents of water from a bare rock, was nevertheless condemned for unholiness and lack of faith, because, under great provocation, he lost his temper. We might think that this was of little importance in view of his great miracle, but clearly God thought otherwise. His severe treatment of His honoured servant was no doubt intended to remind the Israelites, and us, that He puts little value on signs and wonders but great value on patience and humility.

AUGUST 19th

MOSES THE MAN OF GOD   *Reading: Deuteronomy 34. 1–12.*

When Moses stood on Mount Nebo he was experiencing his greatest disappointment, yet at the same time he was facing his greatest triumph—disappointment because his plea to enter the promised land had been rejected; triumph because he was to have the unique honour of being buried by God, and later of standing with the transfigured Christ on another mountain. His humble acceptance of God's severe discipline reveals his true greatness. He had not tried to excuse his failure by putting the blame on the Israelites who had so sorely provoked him; he had meekly submitted to the heart-breaking disqualification imposed upon him, and had concentrated all his concern and sympathy on his successor, Joshua. Moses was surely the most Christlike man of Old Testament times, a true "man of God".

AUGUST 20th

NAAMAN   *Reading: 2 Kings 5. 11–19.*

God's mercy to the Syrian general, Naaman, was so spectacular
that it was to be expected that he would respond by becoming
a true worshipper. What shocks most readers, however, is his
proposal concerning his future behaviour in the house of
Rimmon. Before we begin to denounce this as compromise,
however, it may be good to take note of his virtues. He was
no hypocrite, but openly voiced his difficulties as an officer to
the king. He was a bold witness, who intended his new allegiance to be as clearly seen as the two mules' burdens of earth.
Also he was grateful, ready to give generously to Elisha in
appreciation of God's healing power which he had experienced.
When we can claim similar virtues of generosity, boldness and
transparency we may be better qualified to criticise Naaman,
but we shall probably not want to do so. Elisha certainly had
no criticism to offer.

AUGUST 21st

NABAL   *Reading: 1 Samuel 25. 2–17.*

No wonder that Nabal died of a heart attack. Heavy drinking
and a sudden shock helped to bring it about, but it was chiefly
due to the fact that for years he had indulged in passionate
outbursts of rage. David's polite and reasonable request produced just such an outburst, which both surprised and dis-
gusted him. Nabal's servants, however, were far from
surprised, since for years they had been obliged to endure his
tantrums and had regarded them as inevitable. As for Nabal's
wife, she was forced to spend time and skill in trying to smooth
over the harm brought about by his intemperate abuse.
Nobody dared to contradict Nabal for fear of these fits of
temper; he was wealthy and so could afford to be as rude and
cantankerous as he liked. In the end he himself was the greatest
sufferer, as such bad-tempered people usually are.

AUGUST 22nd

NABOTH   *Reading: 1 Kings 21. 1–19.*

There is little doubt that Ahab would have overpaid Naboth very handsomely in order to satisfy his whim, and many a lesser man would have seized the opportunity to drive a hard bargain. Naboth did not do so, and although he had the law as well as family self-respect on his side he had to pay dearly for his refusal. Today the developers and speculators do not literally murder the innocent small man as Jezebel and Ahab murdered Naboth, but they are still quite ruthless in getting their modern equivalent of Ahab's "garden of herbs". Not that Ahab ever enjoyed this property, for about seventeen years later it was still known as "the field of Naboth the Jezreelite", and in that very plot of ground disgrace came to Ahab's family (2 Kings 9. 25). Naboth may have lost his earthly heritage but he has bequeathed to us the spiritual heritage that principle is more important than money, or even than life itself.

AUGUST 23rd

NADAB   *Reading: Leviticus 10. 1–20.*

There seem to be special spiritual perils for eldest sons. Cain, Reuben, Er and Amnon are all examples of eldest sons who were failures and brought disgrace to their fathers. Alcohol seems to have been the cause of Nadab's downfall, while with others it was jealousy, sex or some other factor, though possibly there is a basic explanation of this common failure of the firstborn. Can it be that those who have the special responsibilities connected with their fathers' names are peculiar objects of satanic attacks? Does the enemy seek to discredit the father by seducing the son? This was certainly true in the case of the Lord Jesus who is called God's Firstborn. Happily in His case Satan failed; no sorrow or disgrace ever came to God as it came to poor Aaron. It was Christ who taught us all to pray to our heavenly Father, "Hallowed be Thy name."

AUGUST 24th

NAHUM   *Reading: Nahum 1. 7–15.*

Nahum means "compassionate", so the strong condemnation of Nineveh may come strangely from such lips as his. Jonah might have enjoyed being able to voice Nahum's fierce exultation at the prospect of the complete overthrow of the Assyrian city of wickedness, but he was not allowed to do so. This was partly because the time for judgment had not yet come, but even more it was because Jonah's intense personal dislike of Nineveh disqualified him from being entrusted with this kind of message. The man who enjoys the idea of denunciation and doom will seldom be allowed to speak in this way. The one who is called to declare God's dreadful judgments is far more likely to be a compassionate Nahum who would much rather run over the mountains with the good tidings of peace. It was the tender-hearted Christ who spoke most sternly of eternal condemnation.

AUGUST 25th

NAOMI   *Reading: Ruth 4. 14–17.*

Burdened with the painfulness of repeated adversities, Naomi returned to the happy harvest atmosphere of her native Bethlehem an empty and disillusioned widow. She added self-pity to the amazed pity of her neighbours and was ready to abandon her name Naomi ("pleasant") and adopt the more sombre name of Mara ("bitter"). Yet all unknown to her a wonderful future awaited her there, and later the very women who had so loudly pitied her were crowding around her and her infant grandson with excited congratulations. Had she yielded to her earlier impulse she would now have had to change her name back again, for the bitterness was past and the future prospect as pleasant as it could be. So the lights and shades of life pass over us all: one moment is pleasant, another bitter, and then the next pleasant again. Only God dwells in the light where there are no shadows.

AUGUST 26th

NAPHTALI   *Reading: Deuteronomy 33. 23–29.*

All the Lord's people are saved, but not all are satisfied. Indeed they cannot find real satisfaction if they seek it other than in God Himself. Moreover they must be outward looking, ready to go to the help of others and eager to fight in the Lord's battles. The people who are oppressed with self-centred cares can never "possess" anything, for they are distracted by frustrations and unsatisfied longings. Those who would enjoy the blessing of Naphtali must first discover and enjoy the fulness of God's favour in Christ and find all their satisfaction in Him. They will then discover that the only way to maintain this satisfaction is to share it with others, for God's cup of blessing is meant to be an overflowing cup. Naphtali was to possess the west and the south; for us there is no direction into which we cannot move with lasting value, provided we keep close touch with the fountain of all fulness.

AUGUST 27th

NATHAN   *Reading: 2 Samuel 12. 1–13.*

The name Nathan means "he gives"; and if ever a man was a God-given help to another, Nathan was to guilty David. Nathan himself must have received a rude shock when he first learned of the king's behaviour, but he was willing to be God's messenger of recovery. In doing so he was faced with the problem of how he could charge David without producing a worse hardening of heart, to say nothing of endangering his own life. After prayerful thought he chose the story of the ewe lamb. It was a flash of inspiration, and it touched David's heart, leading to conviction, confession and cleansing. In our follies and sins the greatest gift that God can give us is a friend who is both frank and tactful, a Nathan who is sensitive and prayerful enough to find a way of appealing to our heart, and bold enough to say, "Thou art the man."

AUGUST 28th

NATHANAEL *Reading: John 1. 45–51.*

If Jesus knew what Nathanael was doing under the fig tree before he was called, He must have known of the contemptuous remark about Nazareth with which he replied to Philip's news. It was typical of the Lord Jesus that He paid no attention to Nathanael's slighting remark, but expressed appreciation of the essential purity of his spirit. It is so easy to counter a sneer with another sneer, or at best with a cutting rebuke which is calculated to abash the culprit. Christ did just the opposite, and soon they were talking not about Nazareth but about an opened heaven. Nathanael must have regretted his rash judgment, but he never regretted becoming a disciple, living to see the wonderful Pentecostal days of the open heaven, when they were all so joyful and so proud of the name Jesus of Nazareth.

AUGUST 29th

NEBUCHADNEZZAR *Reading: Daniel 4. 30–37.*

Nebuchadnezzar learned spiritual wisdom by a mental breakdown, as others have done since. For him there was no skilful treatment or quick relief, but in the end he made a full recovery. The turning point came when he lost the sense of his own greatness, and recognised the greatness of God. How often, with all of us, humility is the first step to true sanity! Until this dreadful breakdown Nebuchadnezzar had considered himself "something", and humanly speaking he had good reason for his conceit. At the moment of truth, however, he realised that all the inhabitants of the earth are as nothing to God, and in the salutary realisation of his own nothingness he found mercy and restoration. Thus for him even a mental breakdown had values, for as a result of it he entered into a right relationship with God.

AUGUST 30th

NEHEMIAH   *Reading: Nehemiah 6. 2–9.*

Nehemiah was not a great man in his own estimation, but he felt convinced that his was a great work. Whenever a man has an urge to do some work for God and responds in faith, then he may be assured that however humble the task may be it is a great work. For this reason it meets with great opposition, as Nehemiah discovered. If he had regarded his work as insignificant he might have yielded to the suggestion that he should leave it for a time to parley with his enemies. He might reasonably have felt that he could easily resume the work when he had investigated their proposals; but the very act of suspending the work and going down to parley would have damaged his relationship with God, and deprived him of his moral authority over his fellow workers. A trap had been set for him, but he was saved from it by remembering the greatness of his task.

AUGUST 31st

NICANOR   *Reading: Acts 6. 1–7.*

The apostles were wise not to get involved in administrative details, and right not to become involved in the strain between the Hebrew and the Greek-speaking groups of Christians. Nicanor was one of the Spirit-filled and trusted seven who handled the matter so wisely that it never recurred. Nicanor's name means "victor" and it seems singularly apt in this context, for the work which he and the other six did meant a real victory, not for any party but for tolerance and commonsense. It is evident that the affairs of the Jerusalem church went forward with a new impetus after the appointment of the seven stewards; the only one who was defeated was Satan, who had tried to use natural differences to divide the Church of Christ. Nicanor and the others defeated him by rectifying grievances and freeing the twelve for their specific work in prayer and the preaching of the Word.

SEPTEMBER 1st

NICODEMUS *Reading: John 3. 1–5.*

If the disciples were present at this nocturnal interview they must have marvelled that the Lord Jesus dealt so uncompromisingly with this leader whose support might have given them some standing in the religious world. He who had welcomed men like Matthew now sent Nicodemus away with the firm insistence that he could only be accepted on the basis of new birth. Nicodemus wanted to bring his own knowledge and religious experience to enrich the apostolic band, but the Lord Jesus could not accept such an offer. Another nameless ruler who wished to contribute his material wealth was similarly rejected (Mark 10. 22). With Christ we either begin at zero or we do not begin at all. Until Nicodemus had learned this lesson there was no alternative but to go back into the night.

SEPTEMBER 2nd

NIMROD *Reading: Genesis 10. 8–10.*

Throughout the ages Babylon has been symbolic of the spiritual kingdom which has trafficked in the bodies and souls of men. It all began with Nimrod, who enjoyed the chase to such a degree that his fame as a mighty hunter became proverbial: the motive power of his kingdom was the pursuit of earthly greatness. The hunter must be merciless, and the hunter of power the most merciless of all. Nimrod's hunting was watched by the Lord, and from that day to this God has observed Babylon's relentless hunting down of all who serve God and attribute greatness only to Him. The chase begun by Nimrod has accelerated more and more and will culminate in universal persecution by Antichrist. One day God will watch no longer, but will intervene and call a halt to this merciless pursuit of the godly (Revelation 18. 2).

SEPTEMBER 3rd

NOAH   *Reading: Genesis 8. 6–16.*

Abel was taken away from his difficulties by sudden death; Enoch was removed from his troubles by miraculous rapture; the third man of faith escaped from impending calamity neither by death nor by being caught away, but by going through. Noah had to endure one hundred and twenty years of rejection, one hundred and fifty days of fearful storms and floods, and then over four months of waiting for permission to emerge from the ark. His name means "rest". All who wonder how a man can live first among scoffing neighbours, then through terrifying storms with the responsibilities of a floating menagerie, and yet be a man of rest, will agree that Noah was a living miracle. His was "the peace of God which passes all understanding."

SEPTEMBER 4th

OBADIAH THE GOVERNOR   *Reading: 1 Kings 18. 3–16.*

When Elijah was hiding from Jezebel he was sustained miraculously, first by the ravens and then by the seemingly inexhaustible supply of oil and meal from the widow's scanty resources. This was an exacting experience, demanding real faith, but it was also very exhilarating. The hundred prophets described here had a much less sensational diet. They were smuggled into two caves and surreptitiously given bread and water by Obadiah, the governor of Ahab's palace. Obadiah was no hero and may compare very unfavourably with the uncompromising Elijah, yet he served God by feeding His servants, a work of real importance. It is probable that Elijah and Obadiah had little mutual sympathy, for they were too dissimilar to understand each other's calling; but each feared the Lord and served His will. No servant of God must misunderstand or belittle a colleague whose course is different from his own: each must be true to God in his own way.

SEPTEMBER 5th

OBADIAH THE PROPHET   *Reading: Obadiah 10–17.*

This book, the smallest in the Old Testament, has a scathing rebuke for those who "stand on the other side" when their brothers are in trouble which they have brought on themselves. In a sense this is a counterpart of the New Testament parable of the Good Samaritan. Esau not only stood aloof when his brother Jacob was in distress; he not only laughed at the calamity; he even helped himself to some of the spoil, and made sure that nobody got away scot-free. In most of us there is a treacherous tendency to stand aloof from those whose behaviour has incurred divine chastening, and in some a strange streak of malice which almost makes them find pleasure in their discomfiture. Obadiah warns us that we shall reap what we sow. Thank God, though, he also reminds the sufferers that with God there is always the hope of recovery.

SEPTEMBER 6th

OBED   *Reading: Ruth 4. 13–17.*

There was tremendous joy in Bethlehem when Obed was born. Boaz had married late in life and so must have been delighted to have an heir. Ruth herself was overjoyed to have become a mother instead of a childless widow. The most excited of all, however, was grandmother Naomi, who claimed the baby as her own, and cheerfully accepted congratulations from all her friends. The only gloomy Bethlehemites were those legalists (slaves to the letter of the law), who felt nothing but foreboding at the product of a union with a banned Moabitess. They feared the worst and, like our modern sticklers for the letter of the law, probably did not hesitate to pronounce it. They were, of course, proved wrong not by argument but by the realities of history, for Obed was destined to be grandfather to the great king David.

OBED-EDOM   *Reading: 2 Samuel 6. 10–12.*

Obed-edom gives us an illustration of reverence without inhibition. The men of Beth-shemesh lacked proper reverence for the ark of God; so did Uzzah; and so, in a sense, did David, who tried to transport it according to his own ideas. All of these met with God's displeasure. Obed-edom, however, was a truly reverent man, not too fearful to give the ark a place in his home, and yet not lacking in dignified respect for the sacred charge. In his case God's pleasure was made very evident, for everybody knew of the special blessings which came on his house (1 Chronicles 26. 4, 5). This Old Testament believer sets a good example to us, who house not the shadow but the substance of God's holy presence. The fact that our bodies are indwelt by Christ should restrain our follies without diminishing our joy.

ODED   *Reading: 2 Chronicles 28. 9–15.*

The prophet Oded had not enough vision to foresee the whole of the Sermon on the Mount, but he had a very clear perception of one of its beatitudes. "It is quite true," he said to his compatriots of Samaria, "that our Judean brothers are suffering for their sins, and no doubt they deserve it. But how can we gloat over their misfortune when we have sins of our own to answer for? We may be more successful than they, but we are no better. Let us show them mercy. Let us help them and send them home again, with thankfulness that God is not also calling us to account concerning our sins." His appeal met with the immediate and generous response of practical help for the sufferers. Oded's beatitude is one which is at times overlooked by the Christians of today: it is, "Blessed are the merciful: for they shall obtain mercy."

SEPTEMBER 9th

OHOLIAB   *Reading: Exodus 35. 30–35.*

Oholiab was not a preacher or a teacher, yet without him it would have been difficult or perhaps impossible for God's message to be received by His people. Oholiab was a practical man, a handyman, whose manual skill was just as God-given as any other, and certainly just as necessary. Every church today is indebted to its Oholiabs, who are ready to use their skilful hands in the practical needs which constantly arise, especially in our contemporary age of electrical and electronic equipment. Such modern Oholiabs have a God-given wisdom, without which they would be as clumsy and incompetent as the rest of us. But they must also have a willing heart given to them by God, the more so as their work is frequently un-appreciated and done in their spare time. Happy the church which has such men among its members, men with both wise and willing hearts.

SEPTEMBER 10th

OHOLIBAH   *Reading: Ezekiel 23. 22–27.*

One of the great differences between the Bible and porno-graphic books is that, whereas such books amuse or corrupt, the Word of God emphasises the repulsiveness of sin. It is not only the physical actions which are condemned, but the cheapness, the meanness and the squalor of this abandoned kind of behaviour. Oholibah means "my tent is in her", which implies that we are not reading of some ignorant unfortunate, but of a woman given an honoured place in a decent man's life, then defiling his home with her unclean behaviour. Spiritually this is what Judah did to God. Spiritu-ally this is how idolatry is always viewed. To give to some other person or thing the place which should belong only to God is mean and ungrateful, and perhaps it takes the shocking story of a woman like Oholibah to impress this truth on our minds.

SEPTEMBER 11th

ONESIMUS   *Reading: Philemon 10–19.*

That a man called Onesimus ("profitable") should contradict his name by robbing his master and absconding will surprise no one, for human nature is prone to such behaviour. What is surprising is that such a man should return to his wronged master, make restitution for his bad behaviour, and eventually turn out so profitable that there was competition for his company and service. If humanism could produce this kind of surprise we might be more interested in it, but instead we turn with relief from mere theory to a practical power which can get inside a man and give him new qualities of honesty and devotion. Onesimus was not unique, but typical of very many whose lives have been completely transformed by the power of the gospel, and who have thus become profitable members of society.

SEPTEMBER 12th

ONESIPHORUS   *Reading: 2 Timothy 1. 16–18.*

Those who have been hard put to it to find biblical authority for prayers for the dead have made much of this wish of Paul's, justifying their exegesis by the presumption that Onesiphorus was already dead. We have no evidence that this was the case, nor need we presume it just because the apostle implied that Onesiphorus would never get his due recognition in this life. Paul had abundant reason for wishing him well, for Onesiphorus had not only helped him when he was a popular apostle in Ephesus, but also when he was an obscure prisoner in Rome. It would have been gratifying for this faithful companion in his trials to have been given some reward in this life, but Paul had good reason to know that many of Christ's servants will have to wait for His great Judgment Day before they get the recognition which they deserve.

SEPTEMBER 13th

ORNAN   *Reading: 1 Chronicles 21. 18–27.*

Ornan (or Araunah, as he is also called) must have been deeply conscious of God's mercy to have offered to provide the necessities for David's sacrifice. He could hardly have done more if he had known that his property in Mount Moriah was destined to be the temple site. "I give it all," he said to David, and would have done so but for the fact that David refused to exploit another man's generosity to provide his altar, being determined to bear the full cost himself. It is a pity that we are sometimes content to let other people make the sacrifices involved in our work for God. We may talk about praying for the needs to be met when really we mean that we are content only to pray while some warm-hearted Ornan does the giving. Unlike this, David insisted on paying the full cost, and was rewarded by God's fire from heaven.

SEPTEMBER 14th

ORPAH   *Reading: Ruth 1. 1–14.*

Orpah loved her mother-in-law, Naomi, and fully intended to return to Bethlehem with her and Ruth. The deciding factor which made her turn back to her own land was the unlikelihood of ever finding a husband in Israel. She was wrong about that. Did she in fact ever marry again? We do not know. At the moment when she went back from Naomi she disappeared from divine history. We do know, however, that Ruth, who was willing to devote the rest of her life to caring for Naomi, was the one who in Bethlehem met a good man who came to love her dearly, and to provide her and Naomi with a happy home. So the woman who put a husband first stayed in the obscurity of Moab, while the woman who put God first found that He gave her the best of husbands.

SEPTEMBER 15th

OTHNIEL *Reading: Judges 3. 7–11.*

Joshua was a great man of the Spirit and a leader in fighting the Lord's battles. Happily when he died the Lord did not abandon the fight, but looked for other potential warriors. He found that Othniel was just such a man and so endued him with the same Spirit so that he could go out to war. Othniel fought Cushan-rishathaim—Cushan of Double Wickedness— and by the Spirit defeated him, so initiating a peace which lasted for forty years; for just as long, in fact, as Othniel himself survived. When the Lord Jesus was endued with the Holy Spirit He too became a warrior; He fought Satan of Double Wickedness and defeated him so utterly that His victory has secured an eternal peace, which will last just as long as He does—that is, for ever.

SEPTEMBER 16th

PAUL AT JERUSALEM *Reading: Galatians 1. 11–18.*

The verb used to describe the object of Paul's fifteen days' visit to Jerusalem means "to gain information by enquiry". Now Paul did not need Peter to tell him how to become a Christian; the Damascus road experience had done that. He did not need Peter to instruct him in doctrine, for he had been in the school of the Spirit in Arabia for three years for this purpose. What he both needed and longed for was to have more personal details of the Lord Jesus Himself. For this reason he made a special journey to Jerusalem to interview the two men who could tell him most about Jesus of Nazareth—Peter and James. We can only know the Lord of glory by learning more of the Jesus of Nazareth who trod this earth. We have something better than fifteen days with Peter: we have all the four Gospels.

SEPTEMBER 17th

PAUL AT ANTIOCH   *Reading: Acts 14. 24–28.*

Paul first went to this church to render it help, but in the end he received more than he gave. The Christians of Antioch commended him to his life's work as a messenger to the nations, and supported him in prayer while he journeyed. He never wrote them a letter: he did not need to do so, for he visited them often. We should note that he did not go to the Antioch church originally to seek their backing for his work, but simply to share with them the gifts God had given to him. Those who go to a church merely for what they can obtain there will always be disappointed, whereas those who go with a humble desire to give the little they have will be sure to find a blessing, and will most probably receive more than they give.

SEPTEMBER 18th

PAUL AT LYSTRA   *Reading: Acts 14. 18–22.*

A less discerning man than Paul might have welcomed the public acclamation offered to him at Lystra, in the hope that it would facilitate his message to the people. Paul, however, refused to be fêted, and was nearly murdered in consequence; in fact his persecutors thought that they had indeed killed him. It is possible that this was the same occasion when Paul himself did not know whether he was in the body or out of the body (2 Corinthians 12. 3). If so, it coincided with his rapture to the unutterable glories of the third heaven. It is a striking possibility that, while his friends were sadly contemplating Paul's inert body, his spirit was away contemplating the glories of paradise. If this was so, it will help us to appreciate the substantial realities of our spiritual life.

SEPTEMBER 19th

PAUL AT PHILIPPI *Reading: Acts 16. 19–34.*

Philippi was an empire colony where Roman citizenship was especially honoured. Why, then, did Paul allow himself to suffer such indignities without claiming his lawful immunity which he made use of later? It may be that in his spirit he sensed that there would be values for God in that Philippian prison, and so felt an inward restraint which kept him from protesting. It certainly is a remarkable fact that when the chains were unfastened and all the doors opened he made no attempt to escape, but remained to explain the way of salvation to the anxious prison keeper. This, to him, was far more important than his personal comfort or safety, and once the awakened sinner had found salvation Paul was content to move on from Philippi. One wonders whether perhaps he felt that in the person of the jailor he had at last found the "man of Macedonia" whose cry for help had brought him to that city.

SEPTEMBER 20th

PAUL AT EPHESUS *Reading: Acts 20. 32–38.*

At Ephesus the soft scholarly hands of Paul became cracked and hardened by constant weaving. As he held them up to the Ephesian elders, he reminded them that his apostolic labours had been accompanied by manual toil which provided food for the whole mission band. Was there ever another campaign leader who did part-time work in order to support the other helpers as well as himself? Not that Paul would ever have tolerated the expression "part-time"; in tent-making or in preaching, his labours were all concentrated on the one purpose of a life lived wholly for Christ. Perhaps that is the explanation of the healing power which was communicated to others from his handkerchiefs and aprons (Acts 19. 12): it may also be the reason why Satan made such an uproar at Ephesus.

SEPTEMBER 21st

PAUL IN THE ADRIATIC *Reading: Acts 27. 21–26.*

On the Alexandrian ship in the Adriatic Sea, Paul had to wait helplessly for those in charge to realise how foolish they had been in persisting in their course of disaster in spite of his warnings. Yet no man is truly helpless if he knows how to pray. Throughout dark days and nights of tempest, while others despaired, Paul continued to wait on God in prayer, until one night the answer was given to him and he was able to speak with confidence to his demoralised fellow travellers. We notice that he had not only prayed for himself and his friends, but also for the conceited captain, the greedy owner, the treacherous sailors and the murderous soldiers. All these were souls "given" to him in answer to prayer. The man who keeps in touch with the Throne of Grace is not so helpless after all!

SEPTEMBER 22nd

PAUL IN ROME *Reading: Acts 28. 11–16.*

No man would have chosen the noisy city of Rome as a spiritual retreat; still less would anyone have chosen a prison cell for the headquarters of a world mission. God's ways, however, are different from men's, and Paul was His prisoner rather than Caesar's. For many years the apostle had looked forward to visiting Rome, but he could not have foreseen the trying, and yet most fruitful, experiences which he would have there. Every Bible student revels in the spiritual wealth of the so-called "Prison Epistles", which continually assert God's sovereign ability to make everything contribute to the glory of His Son. In the original as Luke wrote it, the book of the Acts concludes with the one triumphant word, "unhindered". Paul had proved the irresistible power of God's Spirit in many places, but never more cogently than in Rome.

SEPTEMBER 23rd

PEKAH   *Reading: Isaiah 7. 1–9.*

Pekah was an army officer who led a plot to overthrow Israel's government by murdering its ruler. He then made himself king and entered into a military alliance with a neighbouring state, after which the two rulers marched on Jerusalem. To Judah's king Ahaz, absorbed in news bulletins and fascinated by political commentators, Pekah was a terrifying figure, though to Isaiah, fresh from his quiet times of prayer and communion with God, Pekah was an object of derision who would soon fizzle out like a damp squib. In fact Pekah was soon overthrown by one more military coup, but before he fell he inflicted a crushing defeat on the forces of Ahaz, who was so cowed by popular opinions that he did not take time to listen to God's word through Isaiah.

SEPTEMBER 24th

PENINNAH   *Reading: 1 Samuel 1. 1–7.*

Peninnah had a large family and was inclined to be conceited about it. Instead of taking God's blessings with humble gratitude she talked very arrogantly, despising her fellow wife, and taking care to point out the barrenness of her life and the feebleness of her marriage. This readiness to dwell on the failures and weaknesses of others is all too common among Christians, and probably springs from a false sense of superiority. The Lord Jesus reminded us twice over that in the end the last may be first and the first last. It certainly proved so in the case of Elkanah's wives, for Peninnah who talked proudly found herself set aside, while the despised Hannah was blessed and used of God in a remarkable way.

SEPTEMBER 25th

PEREZ   *Reading: Matthew 1. 1–6.*

There are strange names in this list of Christ's ancestors. All four women in the genealogy would normally have been excluded for one reason or another. And what shall we say of Perez, this son of Judah's shame (Genesis 38. 24–29)? It may well be that the evil began when Judah married a Canaanitish woman, whose first son was too wicked and whose second son was too disloyal to be reckoned among God's people; by a trick Judah was led into starting a new line through his own daughter-in-law, Tamar, Perez being the elder of the twins born to them. The episode is an unwholesome one, but at least it meant that Canaanitish blood was excluded from the royal line. There was nothing but shame for Judah, but there was honour for Perez and, in the end, glory for God!

SEPTEMBER 26th

PERSIS   *Reading: Romans 16. 7–16.*

Was this the first Christian convert from the land of Persia? His name suggests that he may have been, and his description makes it plain that he was a hard worker. All the men and women in this list were workers; they were all active witnesses for Christ, though not necessarily in association with Paul. They not only worked for the Lord but also "in the Lord", that is, in true harmony with Him, doing things in His way and by His Spirit. Persis was outstanding in this respect. Furthermore he was a lovable character—"the beloved Persis." It is a sad fact that very active people are not always people who are easy to get on with; sometimes their very drive and energy make them difficult companions. Persis was not one of these: he was clearly a winsome personality as well as a diligent worker.

SEPTEMBER 27th

PETER IN HIS HOME *Reading: Mark 1. 29–34.*

It is quite clear that Peter was a family man. It must have been difficult for him, finding serious sickness at home just when he wanted to show hospitality to his newly found Lord; so, instead of helping Jesus, Peter had to ask Jesus to help him and his family. This the Lord promptly did, by healing his mother-in-law so completely that she was able to prepare a meal for the party and serve it herself. By the time the meal was eaten most of Capernaum's citizens were gathered around Peter's front door, and many found healing from Christ's own hands. So we see that before Peter went out to work for Christ in the world, he had a testimony to the Lord's sufficiency there in his own home. This is where we should all start.

SEPTEMBER 28th

PETER IN HIS SHIP *Reading: Luke 5. 1–10.*

Peter could not believe that Christ, the carpenter, could teach him anything about fishing: of course He knew about preaching, but fishing—definitely not! In all probability he only let down his net out of politeness, not because he expected to catch anything. Very soon he learned how wrong he had been, as he wrestled with a breaking net and a sinking ship. Now Peter had many faults, but he had the saving virtue of readiness to acknowledge his mistakes. So straight away, there in the water-logged boat, he got down on his knees and begged the Lord's forgiveness. He got more than forgiveness: he got his call to service. Whatever other primacy he received, we should imitate him in this, by seeking to be first in the matter of humility and readiness to confess our faults.

SEPTEMBER 29th

PETER AT CAPERNAUM   *Reading: Matthew 17. 24–27.*

Peter was indignant that anyone should doubt his Master's loyalty to the temple; but since neither he nor the Lord Jesus had any money, he returned to his home wondering how the rashly-promised temple subscription could be paid. The Lord pointed out that strictly speaking He had no need to pay it at all, but then very kindly showed Peter the way out of his predicament. How did the Lord know that the very first fish to be hooked by Peter would have the coin in its mouth, not just a half-shekel (for one of them), but a whole shekel (for them both)? That was His secret. It was, however, a wonderful indication to Peter of how in future days they would be in partnership. The words "for me and thee" must have been a tremendous inspiration whenever Peter remembered Capernaum.

SEPTEMBER 30th

PETER IN THE SIEVE   *Reading: Luke 22. 28–32.*

When people offer to pray for you it sometimes means that there is literally no other means by which they can help you. Christ could have done much more for Peter, even keeping him right away from the temptation. He had a good reason for not shielding him in this way, for He realised the need to focus upon Peter's faith. The inner experience of faith was all-important, so it was for this that Christ prayed. In order that His prayer should be answered it was necessary for all the chaff of Peter's pretensions to spirituality to be winnowed away, leaving only the pure grain of true faith. Satan, however, did not mean to sift Peter: he meant to destroy him. It was the prevailing prayer of Christ which turned the devil's attacks into a sieve, and preserved what was of God in Peter's spiritual life.

OCTOBER 1st

PETER BY THE SEA   *Reading: John 21. 7–17.*

How was it that the man who might have been expected to shrink away in shame from the risen Christ should be the first to plunge into the sea to meet Him? Part of the reason was that Peter had made a new discovery about Christ, as he showed when he affirmed, "Lord, thou knowest all things." It was a wonderful moment in his life when he became convinced that in dealing with Christ he was dealing with God, from whom nothing can be hid. The Lord not only knew Peter's words and actions: He knew the deepest secrets of his heart. He knew his repentance, He knew his faith, and He knew the reality of his love. Those who appreciate that Christ is like this do not try to run away from Him, even though they know themselves to be full of faults: their only concern is to get as near to Him as possible, and to stay there.

OCTOBER 2nd

PETER AT THE BEAUTIFUL GATE   *Reading: Acts 3. 1–10.*

Instead of going through that ornate door to mix with the important worshippers in the temple, Peter stopped to give his time and attention to a lame beggar outside. This man could not possibly help the young church in its new enterprise; he was penniless, friendless and a nobody. Filled with the Spirit, however, Peter was now moved with Christlike compassion, so that he forgot every other consideration in the one desire to share his blessings with a man in great need. The crowds, the sermons and the conversions all resulted because Peter did not make them his primary objective but humbly sought to share with a fellow man the rich blessings which he himself had found in Christ. This Christlike spirit is the true secret of Holy Spirit ministry.

OCTOBER 3rd

PETER IN PRISON   *Reading: Acts 12. 1–7.*

In that condemned cell Peter slept so soundly that the angel could not wake him with words and had to give him a shake. There are two explanations for his calm serenity, each of them involving faith. The first is that he had Christ's own assurance that he would live to an old age (John 21. 18) and was therefore convinced that all the Herods in the world could not kill him. The more likely explanation is that he almost welcomed the prospect of following his cousin, James, to an early grave, since to be with Christ was very far better. If anyone had asked if it would have been better than preaching campaigns, better than miracles, better than conversions and multiplying churches, Peter would have answered "Yes", for he was not in love with Christian work but with the Lord Christ Himself.

OCTOBER 4th

PHARAOH   *Reading: Exodus 7. 9–25.*

Hardened hearts are not often changed by the sight of miracles: Pharaoh's certainly was not. He demanded them of Moses and received them; but although every new sign produced temporary regret, when the danger passed he reverted to his hardened condition. When the final miracle left the Red Sea open before him he had become so reckless that he plunged in to take advantage of the wonder, and so perished. In Christ's time the religious leaders also demanded signs, but they did not profit from Christ's miracles. Later Stephen did some mighty signs, but they seemed to have no effect on Saul and his colleagues. So let us not be downcast if we find ourselves unable to perform supernatural signs, but rather let us cry to God for the greatest miracle of all—the softening of a hardened heart.

OCTOBER 5th

PHINEHAS SON OF ELEAZAR *Reading: Numbers 25.
7–13.*

Phinehas received great praise from God for an action which
was all the more significant because he was willing to act on
his own. Moses had urged the judges to intervene, but they
did nothing: everybody around seemed to be paralysed. It was
then that this one brave man took action, saving the whole
situation by his lone intervention. His move brought him into
conflict with a prince and princess, but he was not deterred by
questions of privilege, or by possible dangers to himself.
He acted boldly for God, and through him God's people were
delivered from death. We need to learn this lesson on our
battlefields, and especially in the realm of prayer. Whatever
others do, and in spite of our conscious inadequacy, God looks
to us to strike a blow for the life of His people.

OCTOBER 6th

PHINEHAS SON OF ELI *Reading: 1 Samuel 2. 27–30.*

Phinehas had an honoured name and a God-fearing father,
but his short life ended in utter disgrace. Young Samuel had
seen the shameful behaviour of Hophni and Phinehas, yet
when his sons were grown up and were made judges by him
they also brought disgrace to their father's name. Clearly no
father can force his sons to have his faith, but in these cases the
failure was not only in faith but also in simple morals—they
were "sons of Belial". Was this inevitable? It is true that
neither Eli nor Samuel had the advantage of the practical
wisdom of the book of Proverbs, so they may not have been
aware of God's repeated emphasis on the need for discipline in
a child's early years. Christian parents now have that book, and
should remember that it is just as inspired as any of the other
Scriptures.

OCTOBER 7th

PHILIP THE APOSTLE   *Reading: John 6. 1–14.*

Philip had a scientific mind; every reference to him reveals him as enquiring, calculating, or inviting investigation. There is a place for such a man among Christ's disciples, for every true scientist is anxious to learn. When the Lord Jesus asked Philip about catering for the gathered crowd he instantly estimated both the quantity and the cost of the bread required, so that Andrew's intervention with an apologetic reference to five small loaves must have seemed absurd to him. This, however, was his opportunity to learn that there are realms of life where mathematics are set aside. In his own hands the five loaves would have been pitifully inadequate, but when they were put into the hands of the Son of God they became abundantly sufficient. This was a new branch of science to Philip.

OCTOBER 8th

PHILIP THE EVANGELIST   *Reading: Acts 8. 5–40.*

What can a man do when he is burning to get out with the gospel but is called upon by his church to care for old ladies at home? Philip's response was to do the task allotted to him, leaving his future vocation to God. He was right, for soon he was released to take the message of salvation to Samaria, to Africa, and then up the coast to Caesarea. Years afterwards Paul visited his home and met his four active Christian daughters. On that occasion no mention is made of Philip himself, so we wonder if he was away, or indeed if he was ever at home for long, since he is the only man to be given the title of "evangelist" (Acts 21. 8). The man whose life is governed by the Holy Spirit need not fear stagnation nor worry about the fulfilment of his vocation, for God will have everything under control.

OCTOBER 9th

PHOEBE   *Reading: Romans 16. 1–2.*

Cenchrea was a harbour of Corinth, about seven miles from the city. Every Christian traveller knows what a comfort it is to be met in a foreign port by someone who knows the local procedures. Phoebe, in addition to her other tasks in the church, gave this kind of assistance to Paul and many other appreciative travellers. She has been used to exemplify the official status of "deaconess", but, since she retained her old pagan name, it is unlikely that she cared for titles. She merits renown because not only in her own church but beyond she was recognised as a helpful sister; this is an honour open to all Christian women who do not need married status or official recognition, but only the Holy Spirit's charisma, to be a "help".

OCTOBER 10th

PHILEMON   *Reading: Philemon 1–7.*

When Paul wrote this letter for Onesimus to take back to his master he knew that the situation must be handled carefully. He was not at all sure that this old friend of his would be prepared to forgive such an ungrateful rogue, even though he expressed repentance. However, he made Onesimus agree to return, then set to work on this letter of recommendation, which clearly proved successful. Philemon was so moved by it that he kept it as a precious treasure. What is more, God was so pleased with it that He arranged to have it incorporated into the New Testament as a unique example of letter-writing. We are never likely to write such a beautiful letter as this, but at least it should encourage us to pray over our personal correspondence, so that it may have a lasting value for God.

OCTOBER 11th

PHILETUS   *Reading: 2 Timothy 2. 14–25.*

All through the years the Church has been afflicted by those who claim to have special insight: for them the obvious meaning of God's Word is too simple, they must have special ideas which sound mysterious. The "Gnostics" were like this, and they explained away the resurrection by saying that it only meant the rising of the soul from the death of ignorance to the light of knowledge. Philetus and his friend no doubt enjoyed the feeling of superiority over their fellows, but in fact their self-inflation was as malignant as any cancer cells in a healthy body. Already some of those affected by them were missing the mark, not only in doctrine but also in holy living. God's people do not need new interpretations so much as a new experience of the power of Christ's resurrection.

OCTOBER 12th

PONTIUS PILATE   *Reading: John 18. 33–40.*

Pilate was in a dilemma: either he did what he (and his wife) knew to be right and so laid himself open to the blackmailing tactics of the unscrupulous Jewish leaders, or else he passed sentence of death on a Man who, though innocent, would soon have been murdered in some other way, even if He were not crucified. Pilate chose the easier way, and, although his feeble question "What is truth?" may sound profoundly philosophical, in the context of his quandary it had a very simple answer. It is right to do what one's conscience tells one: all else is a despicable lie. Instead of this, Pilate chose the way of convenience and self-interest, and he did so to his everlasting shame. No amount of hand-washing could then release him from his place in the company of those tragic men who have lost their souls because they were afraid of the truth.

OCTOBER 13th

POTIPHAR *Reading: Genesis 39. 1–10.*

We know very little of Captain Potiphar, but most of us have met his wife! Many a man as good as Joseph has been caught in her snares, and so would he have been if he had stayed to reason with her or tried to improve her. He acted in the best way for a man in his predicament, never allowing himself to be alone in her company, and running away when this was unavoidable. Potiphar must have known the kind of woman she was, or he would surely have ordered Joseph to be killed out of hand. One wonders whether he might even have been ready to connive at sin between them if he had not been goaded into action by his frustrated wife. In any case he did Joseph a good turn, for perhaps prison was the safest place for a man harassed by such a woman as Potiphar's wife. As Joseph himself later realised, even his imprisonment was part of God's goodness.

OCTOBER 14th

PRISCILLA *Reading: Acts 18. 24–28.*

On such an occasion as this many a married couple might have gone home from the morning service full of criticisms of the inadequate message of that day's preacher. Around their meal table they might have sat with sanctimonious gloom, lamenting the absence of their favourite preacher, Paul, and complaining of the poor quality of the sermon given by Apollos. They might have admitted that he was eloquent, but they would have shaken their heads at his obvious lack of enlightenment; they might even have questioned whether they would continue to attend that church if Apollos were to be its preacher. Priscilla and her husband avoided these negative reactions, and lovingly invited the preacher to their home, with happy results for him, for them, and for the whole Church of Christ.

OCTOBER 15th

PROCULA   *Reading: Matthew 27. 19–25.*

Legend has it that Pilate's wife, Claudia Procula, became a Christian. The only fact which we know about her is that, while her husband was being pestered by the Jewish leaders in the early hours of that dark Good Friday morning, she was in an uneasy sleep, troubled by dreams about Jesus. They had clearly discussed His case, and may even have agreed together that He was innocent. She certainly must have felt very strongly about the matter to have sent this message to Pilate at such a time. She had good reason to feel so uneasy; the pity is that her advice was ignored. No man should be governed by his wife, but equally no man should be so foolish as completely to ignore his wife's intuitions. If Pilate had paid attention to Procula's warning, his own history might have been very different.

OCTOBER 16th

PUBLIUS   *Reading: Acts 28. 7–10.*

Publius had considerable power in Malta, and was probably the representative of imperial Rome, the greatest known human power. Yet he could do nothing for his sick father: in the face of such a challenge he was powerless. Among the shipwrecked travellers who profited from his kind hospitality was a small man, prematurely aged by travel and hardship, who was a prisoner being escorted to his trial in Rome. He found that the father of Publius was sick, asked to be allowed to visit him, and by prayer and laying on of hands soon had him well again. Publius must have been astounded to receive such remarkable help from an apparently powerless man. Paul had no power in himself; he could not still the storm nor walk upon the water, but he was the channel through whom Christ's mighty power first visited Malta.

OCTOBER 17th

RABSHAKEH *Reading: Isaiah 36. 13–21.*

This was the title of a political commissar who tried to argue the inhabitants of Jerusalem into surrendering their impregnable city, just as Satan tries to persuade Christians to give up the fight. But one cannot get the best of an argument with a Rabshakeh. Languages, geography, history, philosophy, economics—he knew them all; and he even claimed to know about God's ways and will. The king's counsel to the people was, "Answer him not", and when he followed up his arguments with a letter Hezekiah did not reply to it, but spread it out before the Lord. He acted wisely, and Isaiah assured him that he could safely leave Rabshakeh with God. The result of this was that when men arose in the morning Rabshakeh, like the other Assyrians, was a stiff and silent corpse. God always answers for those who refrain from self-justification, leaving their cause with Him.

OCTOBER 18th

RACHEL *Reading: Genesis 29. 16–30.*

Rachel was far from being perfect, but she was the heroine of one of the world's greatest love stories. Jacob found that sacrifices which he made for her were not pain, but pleasure; to serve for her hand was not dreary drudgery, but a swift and beautiful dream. His devotion to his beloved Rachel never diminished, and he cherished her memory long after she had died (Genesis 48. 7). This was her greatest triumph: not only to have inspired unselfish love in an otherwise selfish man, but to have held it and enriched it throughout the stresses of their life together. Not every girl who begins her married life as a beautiful bride finishes it by leaving behind a treasured memory; but some do, and Rachel was one of them.

OCTOBER 19th

RAHAB   *Reading: Joshua 2. 14–21.*

The significance of Rahab's story is that she dealt directly with God. The spies advised her to display her sign when they came into the land, but as soon as they left her she placed the scarlet cord in her wall window. She did not wait for the approaching army of Israel, but tied the red line in the window when only God could see it, for her trust was in Him. That trust was not misplaced, for when all the rest of Jericho's walls fell flat there was just one fragment which remained standing. On that fragment was poised Rahab's house with its scarlet sign, which indicated to God that its owner had true faith in Him. Joshua's men hardly needed the red cord: it must have been obvious which was the house of the believing Rahab.

OCTOBER 20th

REBEKAH   *Reading: Genesis 27. 1–13.*

What can a woman do when she becomes aware of the decline into carnal cunning of the husband whom she once revered, and with whom she shared the answer of God to their prayers? Rebekah was faced with this problem when Isaac was no longer governed by God's prophetic word, but only by his fleshly partiality. She reacted in a wrong way when she used carnality as her weapon to combat carnality, forcing Isaac to fulfil God's will by a cunning trick. Although her plan seemed to succeed, it inevitably brought trouble to them all; Jacob was forced to emigrate and she never saw him again. Rebekah's mistake was one which is sometimes made in Christian circles—she met flesh with flesh. How much better it would have been if she had quietly committed the whole matter to God in prayer!

OCTOBER 21st

RECHAB   *Reading: Jeremiah 35. 3–11.*

Rechab produced a family which maintained the simple and abstemious way of life instituted by his son, Jonadab. The Rechabites recognised that they were strangers and pilgrims, and even when the Chaldean invasion forced them to become refugees they did not change their habits. When one is uprooted from familiar surroundings and forced to live in other people's homes, it is easy to relax old standards and sink into a laxer way of living. God gave these men of Rechab an opportunity to behave in this way, but they refused, insisting that they should be allowed to continue the simple life which they had been taught. God was very pleased with them for this. He will be pleased with us too if we maintain standards which He has taught us, even when we have to live with people who have other ideas.

OCTOBER 22nd

REHOBOAM   *Reading: 2 Chronicles 10. 6–16.*

Rehoboam and his young advisers did not deliberately depart from Solomon's procedure; in fact they only intensified his methods. The old counsellors must already have regretted the oppressive measures of Solomon's declining years, for it was they who urged his successor to remedy them. With all spiritual men there are faults which God tolerates because He knows the balancing spiritual values which can be found in their lives. It is all too easy for younger men to ignore such values, while at the same time eagerly perpetuating the weaknesses which God really dislikes. Rehoboam did this, bringing disaster to his kingdom, and many second-generation Christians have similarly lacked the spiritual qualities of their forefathers while reproducing their mistakes.

OCTOBER 23rd

REHUM *Reading: Ezra 4. 9–16.*

Rehum the chancellor goes down into history as the agitator who led the opposition to the re-building of Jerusalem, first appealing for an official veto, and then forcibly stopping the work. Why do such men and, worse still, why do some Christians devote their time and strength to purely negative activities? Like Rehum, they have many reasons to justify their interference, including the specious plea that they are really only concerned for the king's honour; but is this the true reason? Is it not rather that there is in most of us a perverse streak which takes pleasure in pulling things to pieces? It may be amusing to see a child upsetting his carefully constructed building bricks, but it is tragic when grown-up people take so much trouble to prevent positive building for God.

OCTOBER 24th

REUBEN *Reading: Genesis 49. 1–4.*

"Unstable as water" was Jacob's final verdict on his privileged eldest son. Reuben was probably well-meaning, but was weak and easily led by others. The remarkable feature of water is its adaptability to any environment: it can be poured from one vessel to another, whether the change is from a square to a round, or a tall to a shallow shape, and it will always fit into the new container as readily as it did into the original one. This is the element to which Reuben was likened, and it meant that, although Jacob loved him as his firstborn, he knew that it was not possible for him to hold the pre-eminent position which by right should have been his. Inspired by God Jacob rightly reserved this honour for a younger son, Joseph, a man of a much sturdier character.

OCTOBER 25th

RHODA   *Reading: Acts 12. 11–17.*

Some people might judge it unseemly for a female, and especially a servant maid, to let her voice be heard on the occasion of a church prayer-meeting. However, this is the kind of interruption which ought to be welcome at any such meeting, for it was the announcement that those present could stop praying and start praising because God had answered their prayers. So far as we know she was not prohibited from speaking, but what she said seemed so absurd that she was accused of having taken leave of her senses. Rhoda, however, had no doubts; many things she might not know, but she knew Peter's voice well enough. Many times she had listened to that same voice raised in prayer for others in need: now it came to her through the darkness, telling her that once more God had answered prayer. It was joy, not unbelief, which made her forget to open the door.

OCTOBER 26th

RUFUS   *Reading: Romans 16. 13.*

The phrase used to describe Rufus—"the chosen in the Lord"—is as mysterious as it is striking. It is a fact that Rufus had the privilege of being born into a home frequently visited by the apostle Paul, who there met with loving care from Rufus's mother. If this is the same Rufus whose father was Simon of Cyrene, then we know that God chose his father to carry the Cross to Calvary (Mark 15. 21). So it seems that Rufus was chosen to be associated with the historic Cross as well as with the preaching of the Cross through both his father and his mother. Yet these facts, important as they were, do not explain Paul's words. He was alluding to the mystery of God's eternal choice, not only of Rufus but of all of us who can claim that "He chose us in Him before the foundation of the world."

OCTOBER 27th

RUTH   *Reading: Ruth 3. 11–18.*

Hard experience had taught Naomi the secret of resting in the Lord and waiting patiently for Him. Ruth had made her appeal to Boaz and he had promised to act for her, yet she passed restlessly from room to room, looking out repeatedly into the street, and generally made the atmosphere tense with her worry. So Naomi had to check her, and urge her to sit still and show by her quietness that she had confidence in "the man" who would never break his pledged word. Like Ruth, we tend to fret and worry even when we have committed our cause to Christ. Our restlessness seems to betray a basic lack of trust in our great Kinsman-Redeemer: He will attend to our case if only we will be still and rely on Him to fulfil His promises.

OCTOBER 28th

SALOME   *Reading: Matthew 20. 20–24.*

We know from Matthew 27. 56 and Mark 15. 40 that this was the name of Zebedee's wife. It is the feminine form of Solomon, so that, even if she could not be a queen, at least she ought to have been a woman of peace. When, however, she made her request for the special recognition of her two sons, her action was the very reverse of peace-making, for it only helped to fan into flame the already smouldering jealousy among the apostles. The wonder is that all such rivalries and altercations among the disciples and their mothers ended at Pentecost. Perhaps it would be more correct to say that they ended at the Cross, for that is where not only James and John but their mother also shared in Christ's cup. This is really the secret of peace—to drink the cup that He drank and to be baptised with His baptism.

OCTOBER 29th

SAMSON   *Reading: Judges 16. 15–20.*

Although it is possible to discover a number of very striking allegorical allusions to the work of Christ in Samson's strange and tragic history, it is difficult to draw any moral conclusions from his life as a whole. One obvious lesson that we can learn from his story, however, is that it is fatal to toy with temptation. The final disclosure to Delilah of the true secret of his amazing strength was preceded by three false explanations. Apart from being untruths, these teasing inventions reveal that all the time he was at least playing with the idea of telling her what she wanted to know. The moment he even considered the possibility of revealing his secret he was well on the way to defeat. It is imperative to run away from temptation, not to trifle with it.

OCTOBER 30th

SAMUEL (i)   *Reading: 1 Samuel 3. 1–10.*

Samuel was destined to become a great speaker, both to men and to God; his first need, therefore, was to know how to listen. In the first place he had to practise prompt attention to human calls. It would have been easy to have turned a deaf ear to Eli's first summons, but he got straight out of bed and went to the old man. The second time it would have been easier still to ignore the call, for it seemed that old Eli did not know what he was doing. Three times, however, the boy Samuel got up from his bed, in case after all Eli had something to say to him. Those who cannot listen to men are not likely to hear God; unlike them Samuel passed without effort from listening to his master to lending a willing ear to God. These calls had really been a test: from then on he could speak with authority because he knew how to listen.

OCTOBER 31st

SAMUEL (ii) *Reading: 1 Samuel 12. 19–23.*

Although Samuel was very hurt when the people demanded a king, he never for a moment thought of sulking and refusing to help them. He not only prayed for the new king, Saul, in the promising beginning of his reign, but continued his self-sacrificing intercessions for him right through to the end. A meaner man might have felt some gratification at Saul's failure and rejection, or at best might have satisfied his conscience with a few formal prayers. Samuel, however, cried to God for Saul all night before he went to denounce him, and prayed much in heartbroken concern even after he knew that Saul's reign was doomed and a new king had to be anointed. To Samuel it was a sin to stop praying, even for the wilful and rebellious. If this is so then, alas! most of us are great sinners.

NOVEMBER 1st

SAMUEL (iii) *Reading: 1 Samuel 16. 4–13.*

Spiritual maturity does not make a man infallible, but it does make him sensitive to God. It may appear surprising that such an experienced man of God as Samuel could imagine that Eliab was the chosen king just because he looked impressive. It shows that, in spite of much spiritual experience, Samuel was still not able to see as God sees, and so was in danger of being deceived by appearances. The important thing to note is that he refused to proceed with the anointing, being sensitive enough to register an inward check and to insist on seeing the next of Jesse's sons. When all seven had been rejected, he was puzzled but still refrained from action; not until the disregarded David had been fetched did he feel free to fulfil his task. No man can be infallible, but he can learn how to wait for God.

NOVEMBER 2nd

SANBALLAT *Reading: Nehemiah 13. 23–28.*

Nehemiah had many enemies, but none greater than Sanballat:
he was an influential Samaritan of mixed blood, who had only
a superficial acquaintance with the things of God. This
persistent enemy tried every method of attack, particularly
ridicule, threats, deceitful attempts to entrap Nehemiah into
false moves, and even the master strategy of getting his
daughter married into the high priest's family. This ruse to
produce mixture among God's people was the greatest peril
of all, and not to be tolerated by Nehemiah for one moment.
Many servants of God have successfully resisted open attacks
on their work for Him, and then have succumbed to the
temptation to compromise with the world. They should have
done what Nehemiah did—chased the tempter from them.

NOVEMBER 3rd

SAPPHIRA *Reading: Acts 5. 7–10.*

The publicity given to the unstinting generosity in Jerusalem
may have made Sapphira and her husband feel bound to make
an offering in order to maintain their reputation as good
church members. This would have been an unworthy motive,
though even now a common one, if they had in fact given all
the money received from the sale of their land, but they did
not. Instead they tried to get a reputation for generosity while
still caring for their own interests, which led them to in-
excusable deceit. There is always a danger of such things
happening when much publicity is given to donations to the
Lord's work. Had the Jerusalem believers practised the
anonymous giving recommended by the Lord Jesus, Sapphira
and Ananias might not have been exposed to the temptation
which proved their downfall.

NOVEMBER 4th

SARAI *Reading: Genesis 16. 1–5.*

This was Sarah's name during her long apprenticeship in the school of faith. She was to be made deeply aware of her own inadequacy, which is one of the first lessons in that school. She felt so bad at failing Abraham that she suggested he used Hagar to produce a son. She soon regretted this advice, and so learned another lesson—that human reasoning can be an enemy of faith. Then came the final confrontation with the Lord, when her first reaction was to laugh in scorn, for she still had to learn the final lesson—that there is nothing too hard for the Lord. She came to believe this, and so was able to co-operate in faith with her husband, with the happy result of the birth of Isaac. This final realisation of God's omnipotence made her a graduate of God's school of faith, and she received as her diploma the new name Sarah, "a princess".

NOVEMBER 5th

SARAH *Reading: Genesis 18. 9–15.*

Sarah is distinguished from all other women in the Bible by the fact that we are given her age at the time of her death (Genesis 23. 1). Perhaps this is not only a mark of distinction, but also a reminder of how she proved God in her old age. When she was ninety she stopped fretting and scheming about a son, and entered into a new faith relationship with God. It is interesting to note that after Isaac was born she still had thirty seven years in which to enjoy the blessing God had given her. When one is growing old one still has opportunities for proving God's promises, though one may be tempted to fear that future life here on earth has little to offer. Sarah could have been excused if she had despaired in this way. Perhaps she did despair until she was lifted from her dejection by a quiet inward conviction that God is the God of hope.

NOVEMBER 6th

SAUL THE KING (i)   *Reading: 1 Samuel 13. 8–14.*

It is sad that this king, who began in real humility and showed great courage, should have degenerated into a jealous coward. Some have imagined that Saul's case was hopeless from the beginning, and that God never intended Israel to have a king. There have even been those who have decided that in any case he was not "foreordained", and so was doomed by some divine lack of election. The Word of God, however, seems to make it quite clear that the Lord gave the kingdom to Saul and held it open to him, the one condition being obedience. On this point Saul failed to make his calling and election sure, but this was his own fault and not a matter of divine choice. It is true that at one point he had a mighty enduement of the Spirit (1 Samuel 10. 10) but the *sine qua non* of the kingdom of God is obedience.

NOVEMBER 7th

SAUL THE KING (ii)   *Reading: 1 Samuel 28. 11–18.*

Some spiritists are wont to quote this incident because it seems to give some scriptural support to their procedure, but it is difficult to know how anything rational can be based on this blackest night of Saul's dark history. Was it truly Samuel's spirit, a good spirit sent by God, or a satanic substitute? It is difficult to apply any sane criteria to this strange episode which has no parallel in the rest of the Bible. Whoever it was that spoke through the medium, he left no doubts about the suicidal folly of disobeying God, and had not a crumb of comfort for Saul. All the spirits of the unseen world could not and cannot reverse Samuel's earlier reminder to Saul that disobedience and witchcraft are equally repugnant to God (1 Samuel 15. 23). Those who abandon true faith become easy prey for every crazy superstition.

NOVEMBER 8th

SAUL OF TARSUS   *Reading: Acts 22. 1–7.*

At twelve years of age this privileged young Pharisee was sent
to Jerusalem to have the best education his parents could give
him in the school of Gamaliel, one of the most famous rabbis
of his day. This was just the kind of opening which the boy
Jesus would have appreciated and might have found when He
went up to Jerusalem at the age of twelve. Financial consider-
ations made it impossible for Mary and Joseph to permit this
to happen: heaven, however, was responsible for their poverty
and the Son of God needed no such education. For Saul its
greatest value was to make him well-grounded in the Scriptures; this did not benefit him while he was unregenerate but
provided a solid foundation for his subsequent faith and
ministry.

NOVEMBER 9th

SCEVA AND HIS SONS   *Reading: Acts 19. 13–17.*

The Sceva family were unknown to the underworld, which
was all too aware of those who made real spiritual inroads on
its kingdom of darkness. "Jesus I acknowledge," the demon
admitted; he could do nothing else, for the death and resurrection of Christ had struck a mortal blow at that kingdom.
"Paul I am familiar with," he continued. This evil spirit may
have watched the apostle, tempted him, and been baffled by
his holy life; he may have gloated when Paul was downcast;
he certainly trembled when Paul prayed, knowing that the
apostle had God's backing. But as for the sons of Sceva, "Who
are you?" he demanded; who cares for empty words from
men who have no mandate from God and make no substantial impact on the spiritual world? Preaching and praying
are both futile if they are not confirmed by holiness of life.

NOVEMBER 10th

SERGIUS PAULUS   *Reading: Acts 13. 6–12.*

The inscription on a coin found on the north coast of the island of Cyprus mentions "Paulus proconsul", which confirms the historical accuracy of Luke's story. This proconsul was evidently a seeker, and as such was a ready prey for the Jewish sorcerer Bar-Jesus or Elymas, who was typical of those modern proselytisers who vainly promise enlightenment to bewildered seekers after the truth. It is easy to test them by discovering their re-action when salvation is preached through Christ alone. Paul did this, and immediately unmasked Elymas as a perverter of God's truth, which is centred in His Son Jesus Christ. This striking conversion must have been a great encouragement to the apostle at the beginning of his missionary career and perhaps induced him to adopt the name of Paul instead of his original name of Saul.

NOVEMBER 11th

SENNACHERIB   *Reading: 2 Kings 19. 14–20.*

This Assyrian monarch conquered many cities, but he was never able to capture Jerusalem. Naturally he avoided mentioning this failure in his monumental inscriptions, contenting himself with the record, "Hezekiah I shut up like a caged bird in Jerusalem, his royal city. I erected beleaguering works against him and turned back by command everyone who came out of his city gate." The truth is that when Sennacherib turned from greater conquests to the little city of Jerusalem, he met more than military skill and armaments: he met men who prayed and had faith in the living God. Faith was then, and still is, the victory that overcomes the world. Had the Jews maintained this true faith, Jerusalem would have remained an impregnable fortress.

NOVEMBER 12th

SETH   *Reading: Genesis 4. 25–26.*

Seth's name means "substitute", and it was given to him because he was born to Eve to replace her lost son, Abel. It was an exacting task, especially for a younger brother, to have to take the place of such a godly man as Abel, but Seth measured up to his responsibility so well that his own son's birth marked the reappearance on earth of a breed of men who were noted for their faith in God. Thus the Lord justified Himself for allowing Abel to be removed by providing a worthy substitute. Seth is an inspiration to all younger brothers who are called on to continue the work of an older servant of God: they are not expected to make a name for themselves, but they are called to produce a people who are noted for their active faith in God.

NOVEMBER 13th

SHADRACH   *Reading: Daniel 3. 20–27.*

The most astounding feature of the experience of Shadrach is that he came through such terrific fires with no smell of scorching to betray what had been happening to him. It is rare to meet such believers today. Too often those who have suffered for Christ are persuaded to publicise their experiences and so carry around with them the constant reminder of what they have been through. Although the trial is now over they are encouraged to feel that it ought not to be forgotten. Similarly some people who have endured personal sufferings are tempted to harp on them so that others may know how greatly they have been tried. Not so Shadrach and his two friends: nobody would have guessed that they had ever been in fires at all, they seemed so carefree and praiseful.

NOVEMBER 14th
SHAMGAR *Reading: Judges 3. 31 and 5. 6.*

There are two lessons to be learned from the book of Judges, one gloomy and negative, the other inspiring and positive. The first demonstrates the tragedy of times when there is virtual anarchy among God's people, whereas the second shows that at such times God takes up and uses unsuitable and unlikely people, provided they yield themselves to Him in faith. The various judges, who give their name to the book, were very faulty people, while Shamgar, who is not even called a judge, was a rustic character whose only weapon was an ox goad. In his days people could not go along the main highways, but had to creep along small side roads without weapons or the courage to use them. Shamgar, however, kept his ox goad sharp and used it to such advantage that at least he kept the by-paths safe for travellers. If you are not a big enough man to open up a highway it may be that you can help people on the lesser paths.

NOVEMBER 15th
SHAPHAT *Reading: 1 Kings 19. 16–21.*

Shaphat was a wealthy man in terms of lands and cattle, but wealthier still to have a son such as Elisha. At home he had been hard-working, and now the time had come for him to leave all and be entirely given to the service of God. We are given no details of the farewell feast, but know enough of the experiences of modern missionary candidates to appreciate the mixture of sorrow and pride which must have filled the hearts of Shaphat and his wife as they let their son go to God. They may have wondered whether their sacrifice was justified when news reached them of the lowly service which Elisha was doing as Elijah's handyman, but it must have been a great day for them when they heard of their son's experience of the "double portion of the Spirit" and his subsequent ministry of life and power. No father could have a greater joy than that which came to Shaphat.

NOVEMBER 16th

SHEAR-JASHUB   *Reading: Isaiah 7. 1–7.*

The name Shear-jashub means "a remnant shall return", and
by giving it to his eldest son Isaiah put his life's work into a
phrase, for his commission was to inspire faith in a day of
declension, so that the jeopardised purposes of God might be
fulfilled in a believing remnant. Isaiah proved to be a true
prophet, for, after the inevitable captivity, a remnant did
return from Babylon. After the long gap at the end of the Old
Testament it was a vital remnant which welcomed the birth
of Jesus, and again after He had been rejected and crucified it
was a Jewish remnant which formed the nucleus of the
Church. We seem now to be nearing the end of the Church
age; the love of many is growing cold, and there is fresh need
for a faithful remnant. Once again Shear-jashub is a timely
name.

NOVEMBER 17th

SHEBA'S QUEEN   *Reading: 1 Kings 10. 1–8.*

Solomon had prayed for people like this unnamed queen
(1 Kings 8. 41–43). He probably did not know her, so would
not realise that soon after his prayer she would make the long
journey up to Jerusalem to visit him. The happy feature of her
visit was that she found everything better than she had even
hoped for. We who pray for those who spiritually are distant
strangers may well ask ourselves what they will find if they
come to visit us. When they come to our church or home do
they envy our happiness? Do they find the answer to their
hearts' problems? Do they find a new "ascent" into God's
presence? Do they go away with the sense of a royal bounty?
If Christ is present with us in power and they meet Him
among us these things are surely theirs, but if His presence is
lacking they will go away disappointed.

NOVEMBER 18th

SHEMAIAH   *Reading: 1 Kings 12. 21–24.*

Events show that the description given to Shemaiah, "a man of God", was well justified. Rehoboam was very angry with the Ten Northern Tribes for their rebellion, and he had both the power and the will to crush them. He did not hesitate, but ordered a general mobilisation and a declaration of war. Thereupon one simple servant of God, with no title, no powerful backing, and no great eloquence, ordered him to cancel the operation and to accept the situation as it was. Shemaiah uttered no threats; he made no promises; his message to the king and to the people was brief and simple; yet it was instantly obeyed. This is an excellent example of spiritual authority, an authority depending not on any office given to a man or claimed by him, but solely on his life and walk with God.

NOVEMBER 19th

SHIMEI   *Reading: 2 Samuel 16. 5–13.*

Shimei was quick to vent his spite on David when he met him under a cloud, and then quick to speak smooth words to him when the cloud had passed and David was once again a popular figure. So we note that Shimei was essentially a mean kind of man. For his part David neither showed resentment nor acted revengefully, but proved himself patient in defeat and magnanimous in victory, for he was essentially a man of noble character. It is interesting to observe how the trouble in the kingdom caused by Absalom's rebellion brought to light the true natures of these two men, just as nowadays the crises which occur from time to time in the work of God expose either the meanness of those who are like Shimei or the real worth of those who are like David.

NOVEMBER 20th

SHUNAMMITE *Reading: 2 Kings 4. 29–37.*

We do not know the name of this wealthy woman of
Shunam whose only son died so suddenly, but we are told
that he was born to her by a specially gracious intervention of
God. It must have seemed strange to her that such a wonderful
gift should have been removed by death, but she never seems
to have doubted the wisdom and power of God. She was
right in so trusting, for in fact God had only taken him in
order to restore him to her in an altogether new way—by an
act of resurrection. The Shunammite showed the reality of
her simple faith by placing the child's body not on his own
bed nor on hers, but on "the bed of the man of God", so
making him Elisha's responsibility. The prophet accepted the
challenge and there on his own bed received God's answer of
life. Let us lay our dead hopes on Christ Himself, and He will
give us new proofs of His resurrection power.

NOVEMBER 21st

SILAS *Reading: Acts 15. 22–27.*

However carefully a letter may be worded it is always open
to misunderstanding, so it was good that Silas and Judas
accompanied the Jerusalem letter which was taken back to the
church at Antioch. But why were two men sent? Would not
one have been enough? It is a notable fact that the church had
followed this same principle when it sent Peter and John to
Samaria, that the Holy Spirit separated both Saul and Barnabas
for the work of the gospel, and that when Paul found that he
and Barnabas were no longer compatible he did not go off
alone on his travels but invited Silas to be his companion.
This is all in harmony with the precedent set by our Lord
when He sent out His disciples two by two, well knowing
that every man needs the balancing influence of fellowship.
To Silas fell the great privilege of providing such comradeship
for the apostle Paul.

NOVEMBER 22nd

SILVANUS   *Reading: 1 Thessalonians 1. 1–5.*

This may well be the same man who is called Silas in the book of the Acts, and if so he not only shared in Paul's work of preaching but, with Timothy, had some part in the writing of the letters to the Thessalonians. It is possible, of course, that Paul was solely responsible for the composition of the letters and only added the names of his two companions out of courtesy, but it is also possible that they helped him by subjecting the originals to some critical examination. The letters themselves were inspired by the Holy Spirit, but if they contained sentences which were lacking in inspiration who better than these two to suggest omitting them? Any servant of God knows how to value the faithful friends who can advise him not to say or write something which is not truly "in the Spirit".

NOVEMBER 23rd

SIMEON THE PATRIARCH   *Reading: Genesis 34. 25–31.*

One would like to think that Simeon's concern for his sister Dinah was a genuinely moral revulsion from Shechem's behaviour, but it seems more likely that it sprang from wounded pride. In any case his reaction was a treacherous one, and he and his brother Levi behaved so badly that to his dying day their father foresaw nothing but a curse for them both. The tribe of Simeon confirmed his worst fears, and in the end Levi had to make a complete break with his corrupt brother-tribe (Numbers 25. 14). The sin of the Simeonites was significant, for it was the same sexual immorality which had provoked Simeon's original anger against Shechem. It is usually our own faults which we most resent when we see them in others.

NOVEMBER 24th

SIMEON THE PROPHET   *Reading: Luke 2. 25–35.*

Simeon was a true prophet, whose words proved startlingly accurate. As he handed the Babe back to Mary he told her that the effect to be produced by the incarnate Son of God would be the bringing to light of people's innermost thoughts. Christ was to be a touchstone to all who encountered Him. This was certainly true in the case of Simeon himself, for his contact with the infant Jesus exposed his own heart attitude, which was a simple readiness to go happily to his eternal home now that his work here on earth was finished. This was not a morbid death wish, but a confident discernment of the relationship between time and eternity. Men without faith crave to live on, for this world is their only home. The man of faith, however, has great peace in the thought of returning to his home in God as soon as his task here is completed.

NOVEMBER 25th

SIMON THE PHARISEE   *Reading: Luke 7. 40–50.*

Even though Simon's haughty condescension may have been less offensive to Christ than the bitter opposition of most other Pharisees, only His patient love could have made Him bear with such an unattractive character. No doubt the Lord pitied a man who was so loveless and yet imagined himself to be especially pleasing to God. Simon had a built-in sense of his own superiority, and was as offended as surprised at the Lord's apparent lack of discernment or laxity about separation. Simon prided himself that he excelled in such matters, so he had to be told frankly that, far from being a superior being, he was not only inferior to Christ whom he had been insulting, but even to the weeping woman whom he despised. In God's sight men are valued by humility and love, standards which leave the merely orthodox and self-righteous very much at a discount.

NOVEMBER 26th

SIMON OF CYRENE   *Reading: Matthew 27. 27–32.*

Palestine was an occupied country and the Roman authorities could force any citizen to serve them. The sign of such conscription was a tap on the shoulder with a Roman spear. When Jesus sank under His heavy cross, the Centurion looked around for someone else to bear it: touching Simon, a visitor to the city, he ordered him to undertake the distasteful task. At the time Simon probably resented this high-handed action by a hated Roman, yet it gave him a unique privilege, denied even to the chief apostles and reserved for him, a simple countryman. In such ways does divine sovereignty mark out a man for an eternal destiny. Simon's heavy load took him to Calvary, the very place where all spiritual burdens roll away, and we have good reason to believe that this is what happened to him.

NOVEMBER 27th

SIMEON NIGER   *Reading: Acts 13. 1–4.*

Was this the man who is elsewhere called Simon of Cyrene? This Simon was a North African and could therefore have been coloured, as the surname Niger ("black") seems to suggest. He and the other four were preachers, but on this occasion they were talking to God rather than to men. They were not only talking to God; they were also listening to what He had to say. Prayer can be a mere recital of needs, but it can also be much more, when men set themselves to wait upon God and minister to Him, and so give God the opportunity to make known His will. Simeon, called Niger, was privileged to share in this kind of prayer-meeting, and he may even have been the spokesman for the three who commissioned and sent out their companions, Barnabas and Saul, on their mission. Much can be said of what the non-Jewish world owes to Barnabas and Saul, but the important part played by Simeon and his two friends should not be forgotten.

NOVEMBER 28th

SIMON MAGUS *Reading: Acts 8. 9–24.*

This was the Simon who gave his name to the unsavoury practice of simony. His suggestion was a crude one, but what lay behind it, that is the seeking of power in the work of God by means of money, is still possible, though perhaps masked in a subtler guise. Peter's strong denunciation not only saved the church in Samaria from being contaminated by covetousness, but it also shocked Simon into realising that his baptism had not been intended as a mere ceremony but had involved his repudiation of all self-seeking. He certainly needed prayer, but not in the capacity of Magus—the great one—but of Simon the miserable sinner who was in danger of the wrath of God. He was startled and humbled enough to ask the apostles to pray for him, which no doubt they did, determining to put an end once and for all to any idea of a Magus in the Church of Christ.

NOVEMBER 29th

SISERA *Reading: Judges 5. 24–31.*

No Christian can feel easy about this story of Sisera's assassination, but we must remember that the circumstances were quite different from any with which we are familiar, and we must also note that Jael was not an Israelitish woman. In her defence it may be urged that Sisera demanded more than any normal Bedouin's wife could safely concede in expecting her to hide him in her tent while her husband was absent. If we are offended that Deborah sang so enthusiastically about Jael's murderous treachery and even pronounced a blessing on her, we must equally consider what would have happened to Deborah and the rest of the women of Israel if Sisera had won the battle, realising that Sisera's mother would have been more than ready to gloat over their misfortune.

NOVEMBER 30th

SOLOMON (i)   *Reading: 1 Kings 3. 4–13.*

A man may often be known by his prayers, especially when he is praying alone and his request is spontaneous, as this was. At this time of his life, then, we judge that Solomon was a humble and conscientious man. Humble because he realised his own insufficiency, and conscientious because he earnestly desired to be a good king. His prayer brought pleasure to God because he did not ask anything for himself: he sought only those qualities which would enable him to be a good servant to his people. God is always pleased when men pray to be good servants, for it was in His capacity as Servant that His Son glorified Him. When Christians, therefore, follow Solomon's example in praying for an understanding heart they are really asking to have the mind of Christ, and they may be confident that this is a request which God will gladly grant.

DECEMBER 1st

SOLOMON (ii)   *Reading: 1 Kings 8. 54–61.*

This is the first occasion mentioned in the Bible of a man kneeling to pray. The real significance of kneeling is surely humble submission. If only Solomon had lived as he prayed! If Solomon had fallen on his knees in private as well as in public, his life might have ended not in shame but in glorious blessing. His tragedy was not that he sinned—"for there is no man that sinneth not"—but that he never seems to have been penitent. He wrote three books, Proverbs, Ecclesiastes, and the Song of Songs, and in none of them is any place given to repentance. They offer good advice, gracious promises, and solemn warnings, giving considerable stress to the sorrows which must result from sin, but in none of them do we find the penitent and humble confessions which so ennoble the psalms written by his father, David.

DECEMBER 2nd

STEPHANOS   *Reading: 1 Corinthians 16. 15–18.*

This man's name, Stephanos, means "crowned" and it was no empty title, for he was truly "crowned with loving kindness and tender mercies" (Psalm 103. 4). He was crowned with saving mercy, for he was the first convert in that corrupt city of Corinth. We are not told that he had been a depraved character, but we know that before conversion many members of the church had been such. Stephanos was crowned with serving mercy, for his whole family not only shared his faith but also his devoted service to their fellows. He was crowned with sending mercies, for the church chose him and two others to take their gifts to Paul. And he was crowned with sanctifying mercies, for wherever he went people's spirits were refreshed by his loving presence. These are crowns which we may all wear.

DECEMBER 3rd

STEPHEN   *Reading: Acts 7. 54–60.*

It says much for the discernment of the Jerusalem believers that the first two men chosen from among them were such outstanding men. Philip was the first missionary and Stephen the first to win a martyr's crown. All could witness the fulness of the Spirit in him, for his was a life full of divine power and also of divine grace. His power seemed ineffectual when, in spite of everything he could say and do, his liberty and life were taken from him; nevertheless his end was victorious because of the triumphant faith with which he faced his furious adversaries. All of them, including Saul of Tarsus, saw the light of heaven on his face, and they all heard his last gracious prayer. Even if it had never been answered, it was a truly Christlike utterance; in the event Saul himself was the answer, and he it was who became fired with Stephen's world vision.

DECEMBER 4th

TERAH *Reading: Genesis 11. 26–32.*

Terah was a half-way man! It is true that he made a break with his idols in Ur and set out with the express purpose of entering into the land of Canaan, yet he never reached his destination. What made him settle down halfway? Worse still, what made him hold back Abram, the true man of faith, from pressing on beyond Haran? It may well have been that indefinable discouragement of spirit which Satan seeks to exert on all who move out in obedience to God's call. This is not so much a temptation to actual disobedience as the sapping of the positive will to obey. Without this will God's goal can never be reached, for nobody ever drifts into His Promised Land. When the paralysing indecision of Terah was removed by his death, Abram was free to press on, leaving behind that part of the family which was content to stop halfway.

DECEMBER 5th

THOMAS *Reading; John 20. 24–28.*

Call Thomas a doubter if you will: he would have called himself a realist. It was reasonable enough to argue that Jesus could not go into Judea again without being murdered (John 11. 16), but Thomas the realist was also a loyal disciple and was ready to die with his Lord. Again it was sound logic to maintain that since Jesus had died on a cross He could not be walking around in Jerusalem. Call it doubt or call it realism, Thomas had to be true to himself. He had also, however, to appreciate that to God resurrection is quite reasonable, for He is the Author of life. Having grasped this fact and having met the Lord Jesus for himself, he was no longer a doubter but, logical as ever, he perceived in a flash that Jesus his Lord must also be truly God. A Christian's faith is based on solid facts: he is the greatest realist of all.

DECEMBER 6th

TIMOTHY (i)   *Reading: Acts 16. 1–5.*

It is surprising enough to read of Paul circumcising his young helper, Timothy, but still more so to find that Luke has carefully recorded this event in between the Jerusalem decision that circumcision was unnecessary and Paul's journey to publicise that decision among the churches. Paul was the great opponent of legalism, so he must have had a special reason for this action. It could have been to qualify Timothy in the eyes of orthodox Jews, so that he could better witness to them of Christ; or it could have been a simple expression of Christian liberty, an assertion that a man is free to choose to be circumcised though it must not be forced upon him. The essence of legalism is obligation, which must be resisted: the essence of liberty is love, which involves consideration for the feelings of others.

DECEMBER 7th

TIMOTHY (ii)   *Reading: Philippians 2. 19–23.*

Timothy's circumcision was more than an outward formality; he was a Jew inwardly and his circumcision was of the heart (Romans 2. 29). Not for him the self-preoccupation and self-interest which marred the service of so many of Paul's fellow-workers: he was genuine in his self-forgetfulness. This probably explains how a man who was so reserved and frail, and in need of constant encouragement, could conquer difficulties which overwhelmed his more robust colleagues. A man who has nothing to lose always has a big advantage over those who suffer from the tensions set up by personal consider-ations. Although so unlike Paul in most other ways, Timothy was completely likeminded with him in the matter of reckless unselfishness: in fact both of them had this same mind which was "the mind of Christ", the spirit of the Crucified.

DECEMBER 8th

TIMOTHY (iii)   *Reading: 2 Timothy 1. 1–14.*

If Timothy was a typical representative of the next generation, then why was Paul not more worried about the prospects of Christian witness? His many warnings show that he was not without concern, but he obviously felt quiet confidence which was not based on the character of Timothy but on the great fact of the indwelling Spirit. No matter how timid a man or how perilous the times, the Holy Spirit is always sufficient. We do not know exactly what happened when Paul laid his hands on Timothy, but evidently an inextinguishable divine fire was kindled in his heart. This was the vital link between Paul's generation and Timothy's. This fire never goes out: it is the eternal guarantee to the Church of every generation that the testimony of our Lord will continue.

DECEMBER 9th

TITUS   *Reading: Titus 3. 1–8.*

When there was a tough assignment to be undertaken, Titus was the man to whom Paul naturally turned. He could face the judaisers at Jerusalem (Galatians 2. 3), represent the much criticised Paul at Corinth (2 Corinthians 8. 23), or rebuke and set in order the unruly churches of Crete where the judaisers were making fresh trouble. Such blunt, energetic men are invaluable, and a great comfort when things get out of hand. Paul realised, though, that they are bound to provoke hostility, and for this reason he was concerned that strong speaking should be backed by holy living. Unlike Timothy, Titus did not need to be urged to be strong, but he did need to be reminded of the need for graciousness. God is strong; but He is also kind and considerate.

DECEMBER 10th

TOBIAH   *Reading: Nehemiah 13. 7–9.*

Jude's warning that ungodly men would creep in unawares to corrupt the fellowship of God's people is exemplified by this Old Testament character, Tobiah. How many servants of God suffer from the sneering denigration of some modern Tobiah, who attributes to them his own false motives, and calls attention to their conscious feebleness! How many faithful "builders" in God's house are made uneasy by the letter-writing activities of this kind of intriguer whose dupes come with fair words and then basely betray confidences which are given to them in good faith (6. 19)! Nehemiah bore a great deal, but he could not tolerate such a man being given privileges in God's house. Tobiah and his stuff had to go!

DECEMBER 11th

TOBIJAH   *Reading: Zechariah 6. 10–15.*

Tobijah means "The Lord is good". So marvellously timed was the long journey made by him and his fellow captives that they reached Jerusalem on the very day that Zechariah was completing his visions. No sooner had the travellers arrived than the prophet visited them: gratefully accepting their gifts of gold and silver, he made them into a crown for the man who was to be symbolic of Christ, the coming Priest-King. Tobijah and the two others were greatly honoured, for after the crown was taken from Joshua's head it was stored in the temple. It was a great privilege for these men who had just returned from the distant land of captivity to be immediately given permanent recognition in the house of God, and they foreshadow God's redeeming mercies to us in Christ. We agree that "the Lord is good".

DECEMBER 12th

TROPHIMUS   *Reading: 2 Timothy 4. 19–21.*

Trophimus the Ephesian was a close friend of Paul's, as even the hostile Jews of Jerusalem knew (Acts 21. 29). Yet here is the extraordinary admission that Paul was obliged to leave him behind owing to sickness. The Holy Spirit makes no comments and gives no explanation, but simply records the fact that Paul had no miraculous healing to offer to his close friends and fellow-workers, Timothy and Trophimus. There is no hint that he blamed himself for this, or that he regarded the sick men as lacking in faith: he does not comment on their persistent maladies. This, surely, should warn us not to make superficial judgments or pronouncements about the mysterious ways of God's providence. There is so much that we do not know.

DECEMBER 13th

TYCHICUS   *Reading: 2 Timothy 4. 9–13.*

Some people seem to spend their lives running errands for others and to find fulfilment by so doing; and every reference to Tychicus indicates that he was this kind of man. In Britain we have Queen's Messengers, reliable men chosen for their proved loyalty over a long period, and instructed never to sleep until the dispatches which they carry are either safely lodged with a British Embassy or delivered to their destination. It was in this kind of capacity that Tychicus gladly served Paul, the apostle. The great virtue of such a man is his complete reliability; Tychicus may not have been very clever or greatly gifted in more public ministries, but Paul could send him on any errand confident that he would fulfil his task. Spiritually every Christian should be a King's Messenger.

DECEMBER 14th

TYRANNUS   *Reading: Acts 19. 8–12.*

God is no respecter of places. If the synagogue, in spite of its religious atmosphere, had no place for Christ, then the only thing for Paul to do was to move elsewhere. God not only constrained the pagan philosopher, Tyrannus, to allow the apostle to share the use of his hall, but made that very hall a platform from which His Word grew mightily and prevailed. Since Paul's ministry continued over a long period, we imagine that he had the use of the premises during the hottest part of the day when Tyrannus and his friends were resting or sleeping. But what matters a little discomfort when God Himself is present? He can make a cave into a cathedral; He is able to turn a classroom into a banquet chamber. For the Ephesian believers He made the hired hall of Tyrannus into a veritable holy of holies.

DECEMBER 15th

URIAH   *Reading: 2 Samuel 23. 24–39.*

David's honoured heroes are listed in three classes: the first three, then the second three, and then the thirty. Now this makes a total of thirty six, but in fact the number is here given as thirty seven. Clearly there is an extra name, presumably the last, which is Uriah the Hittite. Since Uriah was the victim of David's treachery, it might have been more tactful to forget him. But God does not forget; He brings the hidden things to light. In fact Uriah's name means "The Lord is light" as we can verify from the "Urim" by which the high priest made known God's judgments (Numbers 27. 21). Those who are treacherously betrayed and deserted in God's battles, as Uriah was, may rest assured that their names will not be forgotten. The Lord is light!

DECEMBER 16th

UZZAH   *Reading: 2 Samuel 6. 1–8.*

It is all too easy for those who are familiar with the Lord's work to assume that they have a kind of proprietorship over it. They almost imagine that they can take liberties which are not permitted to others, especially in their intention to safeguard spiritual values. Uzzah was this sort of man. Long years of having the ark in his father's home had made him lose his sense of awe, so that, when it was in danger of being upset, he recklessly ignored the strict command that no human hand should touch it. He meant well; if ever there was a case in which the end seemed to justify the means, this was it; yet Uzzah collapsed and died on the spot. God must be trusted to care for His own interests, and those who wish to serve those interests must learn to restrain their natural impulses to interfere.

DECEMBER 17th

UZZIAH   *Reading: 2 Chronicles 26. 9–16.*

Uzziah's story is amazingly contemporary. He did all that the modern leaders in Israel are doing. He recovered territory, improved fortifications, and promoted agriculture both by irrigation projects and by building armed towers in the desert. He organised highly-trained branches of the armed services and even invented new sophisticated weapons. God prospered him in all this because it was in accord with His own intentions. The same God may cause the present Israeli government to be marvellously helped, if the time for dispensational changes and the restoration of Israel has now come. Even so, they—and we—must remember that He is "The Holy One of Israel". The message of Uzziah to the twentieth century is a warning against pride and presumption: this brought disaster to him and it can do the same for any of us.

DECEMBER 18th

VASHTI   *Reading: Esther 1. 10–21.*

Vashti's dignified behaviour provokes both our admiration and our regret that she had to pay for her strength of character by suffering divorce and deposition. Nevertheless we find in her replacement by Esther the central argument of the whole book, which is that God's hidden providence controls all human behaviour in order that His will may prevail, even in the godless society of our world. The attack on the Jews was not just a whim of Haman's, but a deep satanic plot against the whole nation, and especially against the little remnant then engaged in rebuilding Jerusalem. Esther had truly come to the kingdom "for such a time as this" (4. 14). Some references made by secular historians suggest that possibly Vashti was later re-instated. If this was so, it is an even greater proof of God's sovereignty in timing Esther's temporary advancement.

DECEMBER 19th

ZACCHAEUS   *Reading: Luke 19. 1–10.*

Without condemning wealth itself, the Scriptures indicate to us how unenviable may be the lot of a rich man. For all his prosperity, Zacchaeus was a pathetic figure of restless loneliness and dissatisfaction until the critical day when he met Christ. We notice that he gave away half his capital before he even began to make the four hundred per cent restitution prescribed by Leviticus. He was, after all, a true son of Abraham, the man who turned from this world's offer of wealth to find his real reward in God. Greatly impoverished, Zacchaeus was nevertheless supremely happy. We need not pity him, for that day salvation had come to his heart and home. Let us reserve our pity for those like the rich young ruler who, because he could not bear to part with his money, turned away from Christ and found only sorrow in so doing.

DECEMBER 20th

ZACHARIAS   *Reading: Luke 1. 67–79.*

Zacharias and his wife Elisabeth were a godly couple who could reasonably count on God's readiness to answer their prayers, so they must have been mystified by His failure to do so for so long. Subsequent events fully explained the delay, for their child was to have the supreme honour of being the forerunner of the Christ who could only be born into this world when "the fulness of the times" had come. John the Baptist, as well as the Lord whom he was destined to herald, had the time of his arrival on earth determined by a perfect divine programme. So while Zacharias was worrying about his apparently unanswered prayers, and even abandoning them in his despair of there ever being an answer, God was waiting for the right moment to arrive, and His faithful servant had to wait too. God is never too late—but neither is He ever too early!

DECEMBER 21st

ZADOK THE PRIEST   *Reading: 1 Kings 1. 24–34.*

The Lord Jesus claimed that He always spoke out in the open, and never said a thing in secret (John 18. 20). Zadok was a man who had something of this same open and transparent character. His name means "righteousness", and his reputation was such that Adonijah took good care not to invite him into the sordid conspiracy which he and others were hatching. No higher compliment could have been paid to Zadok than to be excluded from their secret murmurings: his reward was not only a clear conscience (which is no small blessing) but also an honoured place at the coronation of the king. The tendency to secret murmurings and confidential criticism should be given no encouragement among the community of God's people. We all claim to have been made "righteous" in Christ, and we should all aspire to have the same attitude and reputation held by the righteous Zadok.

DECEMBER 22nd

ZADOK THE SCRIBE   *Reading: Nehemiah 13. 13–14.*

Zadok was a scribe, whose work can perhaps be likened in these days to that of a clerk, an office-worker, or even a civil servant. When Nehemiah looked round for some reliable men who could care for the financial affairs of God's work, he chose Zadok among others, and never regretted the choice. In these days when young Christians seeking employment are apt to despise jobs which have nothing especially "vocational" about them, it is good to remember the many ordinary Christian office-workers who have combined a straightforward occupation as "scribe" with spare time dedication to the work of the Church. Zadok may not have attained to any great heights in his profession, but it was no mean thing to go down on the records as one of those who were "counted faithful" by the great governor, Nehemiah.

DECEMBER 23rd

ZEBEDEE   *Reading: Mark 1. 19–20.*

Zebedee's contribution to the work of Christ was two sons. Many give less. Few can give more. Both were active in the prosperous family business, so their absence must have been quite costly to their father, though it no doubt brought blessing to him and has certainly enriched us all. Perhaps the name of Zebedee became less notable in the business world, but it has become honoured in the Word of God. James was the first apostle to die, and John the last. Had Zebedee insisted on his sons staying at home, as many a Christian father has insisted, then he might have become a greater man materially, but he would have missed the true greatness of being father to the two men who spanned the whole apostolic age.

DECEMBER 24th

ZECHARIAH *Reading: Ezra 5. 1–2.*

A preacher's worth is not to be judged by the enthusiasm of his hearers, but by their subsequent actions. If Zerubbabel had arranged special meetings for his people to enjoy the vivid word pictures of his official preacher, then Zechariah might have had applause but would still have been a failure. Zerubbabel was not content merely to listen but was stirred to immediate action, and gave a lead in rendering practical obedience to the prophet's message. Disregarding the seeming impossibilities, the people took up shovels and trowels and got busy, with Zerubbabel as their leader and helper. This is the kind of preaching we need today; and, what is more, this is the kind of hearing which should be given to it. Between them Zechariah and Haggai were able to give messages which were no mere theorising but which really worked.

DECEMBER 25th

ZEDEKIAH, SON OF CHENAANAH *Reading: 1 Kings 22. 11–25.*

When a man is paid to be a prophet, he is always prone to say what his patron wishes to hear, for after all his bread and butter depend on his not offending the owner of the hand which feeds him. Such was the case of this Zedekiah, who possibly had no intention of deliberate deception when he first became a prophet, but succumbed to a lying spirit because of his anxiety to retain the pleasure of King Ahab. It was not just that Zedekiah's words were false: his whole position was a false one and, as Micaiah rightly foretold, his whole world collapsed at the death of his royal patron. No man can be free from the possibility of deception if his work for God places him in a position which has to be sustained by human favour. God's prophets must choose to rely solely on Him if they are to speak His Word without fear or favour.

DECEMBER 26th

ZEDEKIAH, SON OF JOSIAH   *Reading: Jeremiah 34. 8–17.*

This last king of Judah was a weak vacillator who changed according to circumstances, and who asked for Jeremiah's counsel and then ignored it when the pressure of trouble lessened. This incident is typical. When danger was threatening him he hastened to put right the outstanding injustice of slavery which was a feature of the kingdom which he ruled. Then, when the danger appeared to have passed, he permitted the unfortunate freedmen to be enslaved all over again. This is a common pattern of human behaviour. In moments of trouble men determine that they will change their ways, but when relief from the immediate pressure comes they so often forget their prayers and vows, reverting to the former bad habits. True repentance is very different from this, for it leads to lasting changes in the life.

DECEMBER 27th

ZELOPHEHAD   *Reading: Numbers 27. 1–11.*

Zelophehad had no sons, but his daughters were women of such character that they were instrumental in establishing a law of female inheritance, a legacy of justice for Israelitish women. In making their claim they stressed the fact that, although their father had died at about the same time as Korah, he had no part in that rebellion but "died in his own sin". The implication is that he did not harm anybody else by his wrong action, since his sin was quite personal. We would like to know what this sin was, for it is most unusual for evil not to bring hurt to others as well as to its author. We are not told, but nevertheless we are impressed by the esteem in which he must have been held by his daughters, since their request was not the result of greed nor of agitation for female rights, but arose out of a genuine concern for their father's name.

DECEMBER 28th

ZEPHANIAH *Reading: Zephaniah 3. 11–17.*

Of the various kinds of pride, spiritual pride is the most repulsive. This imagined superiority over others is really an indication of how far people are from God, for if they were close to Him they could not but be humble. Zephaniah himself could have found natural reasons for feeling superior, since he alone among the prophets could trace back his ancestry over four generations, and may well have been connected with the royal family; yet he it was who urged the people to make it their first business to have humble hearts, and urged them to "seek meekness" just as the psalmist had urged them to seek peace. His most hopeful prediction for the future was that Jerusalem would see the removal of the haughty, and instead be peopled by those who were grateful for God's undeserved mercy.

DECEMBER 29th

ZERUIAH *Reading: 2 Samuel 2. 18–24.*

David was one of a large family, but his brothers never seem to have given him encouragement or help. One of his sisters, however, was Zeruiah, and her three sons were very active supporters of David both throughout his time of rejection and all through his reign. We might not associate Zeruiah with the devotion and energy of these three brothers if it were not for the most unusual circumstance of their always being called by her name. It is true that in the Scriptures the name of a man's mother is often mentioned, perhaps in explanation or excuse of his behaviour, but in the case of Abishai, Joab and Asahel they are frequently described as "the sons of Zeruiah" as though their exploits and abilities could all be traced back to this mother of theirs. If this was so, then David was fortunate to have such a sister.

DECEMBER 30th

ZIPPORAH   *Reading: Exodus 4. 24-26.*

Zipporah was faced with the prospect of her husband, Moses, dying in the night. She knew the cause of his illness, and that the fault was largely hers, for she had dissuaded him from having their second son circumcised. Now Moses was too ill to be able to do anything even if she asked him, so with her own hand she had to use the knife which should have been used before, with the striking result that Moses was no longer in danger and made an immediate recovery. Zipporah's action was costly to her, as any genuine repentance must needs be, but it brought a wonderful response from God. James 5. 14-16 seems to make it clear that, if there are Christians today who are suffering from physical ailments which are directly due to disobedience to the known will of God, they too can find the same quick relief by decisive confession and the obedience of faith.

DECEMBER 31st

ZERUBBABEL   *Reading: Zechariah 4. 1-6.*

Any man who is faced with the task of extricating a dispirited remnant from the confusion which follows a breakdown in the work of God will realise how badly Zerubbabel needed all the encouragement which God's Word could give him. He was no heroic figure, no gifted statesman, no eloquent orator, but only a small man facing a very great challenge. For him, and for every other man in a similar situation, God has a message of hope, presented by means of the vision of the lampstand and its living flow of golden oil. Success is not achieved by human ability or activity, but by the oil of the Spirit. Do not waste your time lamenting your own lack of resources, for even if you had them you would be no better off spiritually: the one essential is to experience the unhindered flow of the Spirit of God.